STARGATE OF THE HEART

by
Patricia Diane Cota-Robles

The New Age Study of Humanity's Purpose, Inc.
PO Box 41883
Tucson Arizona 85717
U.S.A.
Telephone: 602-885-7909
Fax: 602-751-3835

New Age Study of Humanity's Purpose, Inc.
PO Box 41883
Tucson, AZ 85717

Cover by Sharon Maia Nichols

Manufactured in the United States of America

Library of Congress Cataloging in Publication Date
ISBN 0-9615287-4-5

First Edition April 4, 1994

DEDICATION

This book is Lovingly dedicated to every man, woman and child and every part of life that have ever experienced the pain of not being Loved and Honored.

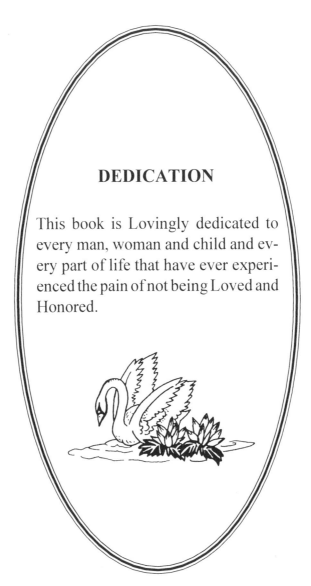

ACKNOWLEDGMENTS

In deepest gratitude and Love, I would like to acknowledge...

Dickie, my sweet husband of 30 years who has given me the opportunity to experience the full spectrum of emotions. And, who now, as we expand our Love and grow together, continually lifts me into higher Octaves of Bliss, Ecstasy, Wonder and Awe. I Love you!

Joao, my son, who is experiencing the difficult challenges of this Earthly schoolroom of learning and is daily growing in strength, courage, integrity and Love. I Love you!

Victoria, my daughter, who has always demonstrated to me what the open Stargate of the Heart really means. Her capacity for Love and Compassion fills my Heart with joy. I Love you!

Kay Meyer, my dear friend and co-worker, who works endlessly to keep our Spiritual work logistically manifesting in the world of form. She continually embraces me in the balance and support I need to keep me centered as we are catapulted through the paradigm shifts into the New Heaven and the New Earth. I Love you!

The selfless volunteers who give of the very substance of their Beings to propel our work into the hands and use of anyone who might benefit from it: Margy Vaughan, Mona Hoover, Peter and Karen

McGeoghegan, Jim McAndrew, Sharon Nichols, Evelyn Copas, Rhea Loren, Kathy Deal, Marjie Anderson, Jack Hightower, Jeannie Graham, Sue Larson, Jeanette Des Lauriers, Peaches, Gordon Fritz, Maria Seri, Albert Kaukaras, Pam Larkins, Liesel and Bill Hack and all of the other precious Lightworkers that assist us physically, financially and Spiritually. I Love you!

Dylan and Hayden, my grandsons, who are continual catalysts for my laughter, fun, joy and Love. I Love you!

All of the rest of my Earthly Family and my Heavenly Family, those who Love me, guide me, encourage me, teach me, support me, assist me and fill the cup of my consciousness with the glory of Divinity in all Its forms. I Love you!

TABLE OF CONTENTS

CHAPTER ONE

WHAT IS LOVE?

The single most important aspect of our personal transformation is the opening of our Heart. Intellectually we all want to have an open Heart, and we want to experience Loving ourself and Loving others. Unfortunately, we have often suffered the excruciating pain of rejection, abandonment, neglect, abuse, dysfunctional families, infidelity, loneliness and other atrocities that have caused us to close our Heart Center down, and we have numbed ourself as a survival mechanism. Because of the pain of our past, we are terrified to trust again, and we are fighting tooth and nail to protect ourself from having to go through the agony of lost Love. From outer appearances, it seems that the only way to avoid the possibility of getting hurt is to not allow ourself to Love in the first place. Consequently, we have created an elaborate game of self-deception and denial to convince ourself that we are happy in spite of the fact that we have shut down our Heart and are blocking our feelings. In some instances, we have tricked ourself into believing we are allowing ourself to really Love when, in fact, our feelings are being conjured up in our mind and not in our Heart. When we do this, our relationships become intellectual and superficial instead of Loving and emotional. This seems less threatening, and we feel safer, but the truth is, by *thinking* Love instead of *feeling* Love, we cheat ourself out of the *most* glorious experience we are capable of having on the Earth plane, and actually, in the Universe.

During this Cosmic Moment of Earth's rebirth, we are being given a unique opportunity to reopen the Stargate of our Heart in an atmosphere of protection, security and Eternal Hope. This is not only a sacred opportunity, it is a powerful gift from God, and it is a very necessary, critical part of Earth's Ascension into the Light. In order to appreciate that fact, we need to reach into the Octaves of Illumined Truth and strive to grasp the knowledge, wisdom and understanding of just what Love really is.

We've heard all of the expressions: God is Love; Love is all there is; Love is letting go of fear; Love is. But, in most instances, these seem like lofty platitudes and not tangible realities. Love is something we've heard the poets and songwriters expound on since the beginning of time, and yet it is still a very misunderstood, and often elusive, concept.

First of all, we must explore the scientific laws that govern Love. Love is not the sentimental, impractical, surface affection that most people have given it credit for. It is literally the cohesive power of the Universe, and it is the vibration of Love that creates the gravitational pull that holds the elements of the Earth together and holds the Planets, the Stars and the Suns of this Universe in their proper orbits. Love is the central building block of all manifest form.

Love embraces, within its sphere of radiation, all of the other positive qualities of life. It embraces faith, kindness, hope, patience, charity, forgiveness, mercy, compassion, unselfishness, courage, peace, contentment, happiness, joy, beauty, wellbeing, opulence and friendship, to name just a few.

Love is a scientific law. It is a principle. In our own individual life, Love is a decision, a consciously maintained attitude of radiation or expression. The aura of Love is Light, and if we draw this force into our life and consciously surround ourself with this vibration, we can be a peace commanding presence, no matter where we are. Love is all encompassing, and the magnitude of its significance in our life is incomparable.

The essence of Love...pure, strong, gentle, complete and unconditional...is the vibration from which we were born out of the Heart of God and the vibration through which we must evolve and Ascend back into the Heart of God. The frequency of Love has no bonds, no barriers, no conditions. Within the infinite Power of Love there is no pain or sorrow, no lack or limitation. It contains within its essence our full potential to rise above all human conditions, all self-inflicted suffering, all manner of chaos, confusion, hopelessness and despair. Love heals the illusion of separation. It rejuvenates, revitalizes and makes whole all it embraces. Love is the single greatest source of forgiveness, and it is the impetus of our FREEDOM and LIBERATION from all of our Earthly woes.

Through Love, we are drawn up into the realization of our own Divinity. Within the wisdom of Love we know that every person holds a unique thread in the Tapestry of Life. Every thread is necessary to the fulfillment of the Divine Plan on Earth. As we tap the frequencies of Love, we begin to experience gratitude for all of the blessings of God that contribute so generously to our Earthly pilgrimage. Within the flow of this mighty force, our faith in ourself is renewed, and we once again perceive ourself as a valuable human being. As Love pours physically and tangibly through the Stargate of our Heart, never again will we say, "What good can I possibly achieve? What value am I? What difference can one soul possibly make?" We will recognize those thoughts to be a sacrilege. God has chosen us to fulfill a portion of the glorious Divine Plan on Earth, and He has asked that we release the unique perfume and music of our Being to bless all life. Something sacred is hidden in each of our souls that has never been known by another, some beautiful manifestation of life which our God Presence alone can externalize. It is time for all Humanity to accept this truth.

There has been so much written about Love that it has almost become a cliché, but Love in its purity is the mightiest force in the Universe. Love is the fulfillment of the Law because there is no power that can deny it or fail to respond to its call. If we tap the Heart of God and magnetize forth the peaceful radiation of impersonal Love, all the good of the Universe will flow into our hands and use. THAT is the power of Love.

When we truly experience the vibration of Love, we will recognize it as the most priceless element in all existence; we will perceive it as a dynamic living force. Love is the vehicle upon which all Light is carried into form. It transcends time and space. It is Spiritual and all powerful.

As Love is breathed into the world of form from the Heart of our Father-Mother God, it carries through the Heart Center of each soul the Divine Light that dispels all gloom and darkness. It banishes decay, misery and evil. It overcomes fear and separation. Negativity and discord cannot abide in the Presence of Love, for this Sacred Essence is a force of unlimited and unspeakable power. Love is a creative force that is ALWAYS constructive and beneficial. It exalts and glorifies.

Love is endowed with a deep vision that peers beyond the scars and blemishes on the surface. Its healing penetrates all exteriors to behold the truth of each soul, the reality of each experience. Love pierces beyond the visible into the innermost depths of perfection and finds its resting place there.

Our purpose and reason for being is to be the bearer and transmitter of Love. This Sacred Essence, which renews all to everlasting life, is the key to EVERY door.

As the cohesive power of the Universe, Love binds into form all physical matter, every atom and particle of life. It holds families together—the world and the entire Universe. Without Love, all physical substance would disintegrate into unformed, primal energy. When we eliminate Love from our life we, too, begin to disintegrate and fall apart. When we incorporate Love into every aspect of our life, we experience a cohesiveness and success beyond the comprehension of our finite mind.

With the fully developed God-given faculty of Love, we have the power to create whatever our Spiritual vision of Love beholds. Our Love will amplify the Love in the people around us, and those people will begin to experience the Glory of God as the Light of Love expands within their own Hearts. This Celestial Song of Love reverberating through every Heart is the greatest gift from God available to us on Earth.

As Love and Light flow into Earth through the Stargate of our Heart, we realize that nothing is impossible.

As we develop this perfect gift of Love, our old stagnant beliefs and patterns begin to crumble, and the Divine Ideas from the Mind of God fill our consciousness. Our whole Being assumes a new vitality, beauty, purpose and meaning. Compassion replaces condemnation; forgiveness replaces accusation; healing replaces disease; abundance replaces limitation and happiness replaces sadness. As we are filled to overflowing with the essence of Love, it begins to radiate out through every cell of our physical body, and we become vibrantly beautiful. Our hands, radiating forth Love, bless all they touch; our eyes, seeing through Love, perceive only perfection in all life; our ears, filled with Love, hear the music of the spheres; and our nostrils, breathing Love, inhale the fragrance of the Holy Spirit. Thus, we become renewed and Divine. In this exalted state of Love, we speak with wisdom, compassion, tenderness and understanding.

Then we will know as never before: *"Though I speak with the tongues of men and of Angels and have not Love, I am as a sounding brass or a clanging cymbal. And though I have the gift of prophecy and understand all mysteries and all knowledge and have all faith so I could remove mountains but have not Love, I am nothing."*

Now, with greater insight and a new level of awareness, we realize Love is the highest attribute of the human soul. It is the most vital energy required for our Spiritual attainment, and the further we have advanced on the ladder of evolution, the more spontaneous and far-reaching will be our expression of Love.

In our time of need, Love is available to assist us as a positive, concentrated action. We receive it according to our capacity to *accept* it at the time of our call.

Through Love, we have constancy in the most trying of circumstances, and we are able to respond at the moment when it is needed most.

As we master Love, we continually pour forth our full-gathered momentum of this Divine Gift for the good of ALL. With Love we experience, with deeper understanding, **a Oneness and Reverence for all life.**

CHAPTER
TWO

TRUSTING ENOUGH
TO OPEN YOUR HEART AGAIN

Some very wonderful things have occurred on Earth recently, and hopefully the knowledge of the Divine Intervention we are receiving now, and the overwhelming success of our progress into the Light will give each of you the courage you need to TRUST enough to open your Heart again. It is impossible for us to fulfill our purpose and reason for being on Earth with a closed Heart, and yet, the majority of people all over the Planet have closed their Heart to some degree with each and every painful experience. This has been a survival mechanism of the lower human ego, that aspect of our personality that functions out of fear. But, when we truly understand the significance of our Heart Center, we will realize just how crucial it is for us to put forth the effort and take what feels like a frightening risk, in order to open our Heart again.

In the beginning, prior to what we call the "fall of man," our Heart Center was a magnificent open portal through which the Divine Love Nature of God continually poured into our life experience. Our God Self (also called our Holy Christ Self) was anchored in our Heart, and the radiance of this Divine Presence pulsated through the open portal and enveloped our four lower bodies.

Through the open Stargate of our Heart, our God Presence was able to continually reflect all of the Divinity of God from the Realms of Perfection into Its third dimensional Earthly experience. This was accomplished through a two-fold pulsation of Light. One pulsation was the *inbreath,* which allowed us to absorb and assimilate the frequencies of the higher Realms of Perfection, and the second pulsation was the *outbreath,* which allowed us to radiate and expand the frequencies of God's Perfection into the world of form. On every *inbreath* our Holy Christ Self Who was anchored in our Heart, reached up in consciousness into the Realms of Perfection, assimilating all of the Light of God It could absorb. On every *outbreath* our Holy Christ Self radiated God's Perfection through the open Stargate of our Heart and expanded It into the world of form flooding all of our Earthly experiences with Divine Light.

As our God Presence progressed through Its third dimensional Earthly school of learning, mastering the creative faculties of thought and feeling, each *inbreath* reached into new heights of Divinity, and each *outbreath* bathed the Earth with stronger pulsations of God's Perfection. Because of this dual activity, our Heart Center is both a portal through which we can reach up into the pure land of God's boundless splendor and infinite Light, as well as a portal through which the boundless splendor of God's precious Light can be projected into Humanity and the physical plane of Earth.

In the beginning, prior to the "fall," we were very aware of the importance of maintaining an open Heart Center, and we were connected with the Realms of Truth and Knowledge in a way that prevented us from experiencing the pain and fear that eventually caused us to close down our Heart Center. At that time, we knew we were multi-dimensional Beings functioning CONSCIOUSLY in all dimensions simultaneously. Through the open Stargate of our Heart, we were in constant communion with the highest aspects of our God Presence and all other facets of our existent past, present and future as well. I know, with the limited perception we experience now, this seems a little bit mind boggling, but remember, it is only in this limited third dimensional reality that there exists such a thing as time and space.

Perhaps it will help to envision our God Presence as a blazing Sun of Light pulsating with the full-gathered momentum of the Causal Body of our Father-Mother God. This luminous Sun Being is our true reality, and It interpenetrates all octaves and dimensions of existence. It is One with the Divine Mind and Heart of God. Now, in order to experience a third dimensional life, which in our connotation means physical embodiment on Earth, our God Presence projects a minuscule portion of Itself, the equivalent of one Ray from Its massive Sun into a stepped down version of Itself known as a Holy Christ Self. The purpose of a third dimensional experience is to give our God Presence the opportunity to learn to become a co-Creator with our Father-Mother God by becoming Master of energy, vibration and consciousness through the use of free will. This occurs most effectively within the denser constraints of a time and space reality and through the use of our creative faculties of thought and feeling. Thus, our Holy Christ Self created from unformed Primal Light Substance the vehicles It would use to learn the lessons of co-Creation. It created a physical body, an etheric body, a mental body and an emotional body. These vehicles were to be under the full dominion and authority of the Holy Christ Self Who was, in turn, to be under the full dominion and authority of our God Presence. A multi-dimensional communication system was instituted that was designed to keep the Holy Christ Self in constant communion with our God Presence and with all of the other aspects of ourself and our many realities. This communication system could be described as an incredibly elaborate version of the fiber optic system we now use for our communication on Earth.

Prior to the fall of Humanity, the Twelve Solar Aspects of Deity that pulsate as the Causal Body of God were woven as strands of Light into every single facet of our Being. This Divine Light contains all of the wisdom, knowledge and truth held in the Mind of God. This Light also contains within It the Divine Blueprint for our sojourn into matter, and It contains the totality of who we are, why we are here and the full potential of all we will ever become. In order to transmit this knowledge and wisdom into the consciousness of our limited third dimensional time and space reality, Twelve Solar Strands of DNA were created and woven into a Twelve-fold Helix of Sacred Fire. These Twelve Solar Strands of DNA were designed to be the "fiber optic" system that guaranteed the continual open communication between our multi-dimensional God Presence—our radiant Sun Being—and our Holy Christ Self Who was abiding in the third dimension.

The Stargate of the Heart was actually the open portal through which the Light of the Twelve Solar Aspects of Deity continually poured to sustain and energize the Twelve Solar Strands of DNA. The pulsations of the inbreath and outbreath of the Holy Christ Self, through the Stargate of the Heart, served as a Cosmic generator to keep the Solar Strands of DNA connected to the source of our God Presence.

Tragically, as we began to use our free will and our creative faculties of thought and feeling in ways that were not in alignment with Divine Will, we created fragmented frequencies of discord and confusion that caused us hurt and pain. These unfamiliar feelings scared us, and we began closing the Stargate of our Heart, so we wouldn't *feel* so much. As less energy flowed through our Heart Center, the Twelve Solar Strands of DNA began to short circuit. Our communication system became flawed, which caused additional fear that made us close our Heart Center even more. As we fell into denser and denser octaves of vibration, the Twelve Solar Strands of DNA began to fray and disconnect. Over aeons of time, our communication with our God Presence continued to deteriorate, and we became immersed in a veil of maya and human miscreation. We continued degenerating until there were only two strands of DNA left intact, barely enough to sustain brain consciousness.* We became totally disconnected from the Realms of Illumined Truth and Knowledge at that point, and we began to perceive the limited time and space continuum of the physical plane as our only reality. We believed that we were just our physical bodies, and the concept of being a Son or Daughter of God was beyond our comprehension. We accepted the illusion that the single

---

The two remaining strands of DNA appear as the double helix of DNA our scientists have now discovered.

minuscule Ray from our God Presence which sustains our Holy Christ Self was our total Being instead of the massive Sun we actually are.

When we started to perceive the physical plane as our only reality, we also started to believe that our only source of Love was someone in the physical plane. That, in a nutshell, is the cause and core of all of our dysfunctional behavior patterns in relationships, and it is why we have closed our Heart Center down so effectively and are terrified to risk opening it up again. When we truly believe that our only source of Love is another person, then we become desperate, needy, possessive, obsessive and co-dependent. Consequently, our relationships are usually nightmares instead of what we want them to be. Each time we experience a horrific relationship, we vow that we will never set ourself up to be hurt that way again. The only way we think we can do that is by convincing ourself that we don't need Love and by suppressing and denying all of the longings we have for Love, companionship, communication, tenderness and sharing. We suppress our physical needs for closeness and sex as well, until we actually become numb and unfeeling. That is when we try to Love with our brain instead of our Heart, and we talk ourself into *thinking* Love instead of *feeling* Love. That feels a whole lot safer and gives us permission to deny the fact that we have closed down our Heart Center. Then we can rationalize ourself into being alone or being in relationships that don't demand our emotional Heart Love. This may feel less threatening, but we are reneging on our reason for being on Earth in the first place, and we are blocking and delaying our growth and self-mastery.

I want to assure you that we can only get away with that cop-out temporarily. Our God Presence will put us in situations again and again and again until we finally "get it" and realize we are not going to be allowed to remain closed down and numb forever. The very difficult part of this process is that our God Presence continually works through our Holy Christ Self to get us to start feeling again. Since we are so afraid of being hurt, we normally don't allow ourself to feel the positive emotions of Love and trust or happiness. The end result is the only thing we let ourself feel is pain, so we keep drawing dysfunctional relationships into our life over and over again.

We must start waking up to the fact that people in the physical plane are *NOT* our *SOURCE OF LOVE*. It is wonderful to have harmonious, fulfilling, Loving relationships, but they need to be the "icing on the cake," not the *source* of our Love. When we allow the Stargate of our Heart to open and we begin drawing our Love from our true source, our Father-Mother God, then never again can a person leave us and make us feel totally void of Love. We may still feel sadness and loss, but it will not be the all-consuming life or death agony of rejection that we have experienced in the past.

I know everyone is longing to believe they can perpetually experience the bliss of God's Divine Love, but we have been so disconnected from It for so long we just don't trust that we will ever be able to safely open our Heart to It again. Well, fortunately, God and the entire Company of Heaven know exactly how difficult it is for us to trust again. Yet, trust again we must if we are going to fulfill our Divine Plan and the Divine Plan of Beloved Mother Earth. Due to the urgency of the hour, we are receiving more assistance than ever before from the Realms of Illumined Truth and Perfection to help us in this very frightening, but incredibly glorious, process of opening the Stargate of our Heart.

OPENING THE HEART
IN AN ATMOSPHERE OF SAFETY

We are in the midst of a greatly empowered span of time known as a Window of Opportunity. Because of the increase and acceleration of Divine Light flowing into the Earth, we have the ability to change our behavior patterns and transform our life far more painlessly than ever before. There is an expression that says, "Cosmic Moments come, and Cosmic Moments go." If we don't grasp the opportunities presented during this Cosmic Moment, we may never again be given the chance to move as effortlessly into the Light. It is clearly perceived by our Father-Mother God and the entire Company of Heaven that Humanity needs assistance and encouragement from on High in order to dare to trust enough to allow our Hearts to open. Several inner and outer world plans have been set into motion to relieve our fear and the resistance to opening our Heart Center. These plans began being implemented in 1993, which carried the vibration of the master number 22. A 22 vibration carries the frequency of Power on all Planes and the ability to change the course of history. We also experienced a rare conjunction in 1993 between the Planets Neptune and Uranus that occurs every 171 years. The activities of Light that were initiated in 1993 are daily and hourly building in momentum, and even if we weren't consciously aware of what was happening at the time, we can *now* tune into these ever-expanding Forcefields of Light and benefit from the Divine Gifts being given to us by God.

I would like to share with you some of the specifics of what occurred in the initial anchoring of Divine Light in 1993, so that your *inner knowing* will project into your conscious mind the *truth* of this Cosmic Moment.

1993 was a God Victorious year in which every man, woman and child was, at long last, reunited in the Realms of Cause with their true God Reality, the highest aspect of their Holy Christ Self, the Solar Christ Presence. Our self-inflicted separation from our own Divinity has been healed, and we now have the unique opportunity of becoming the Sons and Daughters of God we are destined to be.

I know this truth is a little hard for us to accept when we look at the difficult experiences surfacing in our daily life. In some instances, our life even seems to be getting worse. This is happening for a few reasons. First of all, any area of our life that is not reaching its highest level of potential is being pushed to the surface by our God Presence, so that we can clearly perceive it and correct it. This is having the effect of exacerbating the challenges we are going through. In some instances, financial problems are getting worse; dysfunctional relationships are becoming more unbearable; diseases are more complicated; jobs are less fulfilling; addictions are more compulsive; depression is more severe; fear is more agonizing; low self-esteem and unworthiness seems more justifiable; pain and suffering are more intense and on and on ad infinitum. This is happening to jolt us out of our numbed state of mass hypnosis. We are so used to being miserable that we have accepted the negative things happening to us as an unavoidable, *normal* part of our Earthly experience. But, in truth, nothing could be more *abnormal* than the wretched state Humanity has created on Earth. These painful situations are being amplified to get our attention, and they are becoming intolerable, so we will focus on doing something about them.

Another reason things seem to be getting worse, even though we have reunited with our Solar Christ Presence, is because we're being given the opportunity to Transmute the maximum negativity that Karmic Law will allow. Consequently, we have volunteered at Inner Levels to Transmute many, many lifetime's worth of our own negativity in a very short period of time. We are being given the maximum returning negative energy that we can withstand. This sometimes seems like more than we can handle from our lower human perspective, but our God Presence will *never* give us more than we are capable of Transmuting.

The final reason things seem so hard at the present time is because the Lightworkers have been granted permission, for the very first time on Earth, to Transmute mass karma. This means that we are being allowed to Transmute the negativity created by our fellow Human Beings who are so buried in their human effluvia that they can't get their heads above the mud puddle of chaos and confusion long enough to do it for themselves. We have actually volunteered at Inner Levels to Transmute not only our own misqualified energy, but the misqualified energy of the masses as well. This is truly a gift of selfless service that is immeasurably appreciated by the Heavenly Realms.

Whenever we expend our precious life energy to benefit any aspect of God's creation, additional assistance is granted to us from on High to enhance our effectiveness and make our work and our life easier. ***Such glorious assistance is now being granted.***

In order to ease our pain and move us very quickly through the negative challenges we are going through, we are being given an opportunity of unprecedented mercy and compassion. Our Father-Mother God is opening a door to *Limitless Solar Transmutation* that has never before been experienced in any physical dimension. This is a frequency of the Violet Transmuting Flame beyond anything we have *ever* been capable of withstanding. It is a frequency of Divine Solar Light from the Causal Body of God that will instantaneously Transmute back into perfection anything in Its path. It reaches into the cause, core, effect, record and memory of every frequency of vibration that is less than God's Perfection and Transmutes that negative condition back into its original Divine Blueprint. This Sacred Gift is being released on Earth because of the need of the hour and the Cosmic Moment at hand. This is truly the Divine Intervention we have been told would occur during Earth's final purge and cleansing.

This is the Divine Intervention that will move this Planet and all Her life quickly into the Octaves of Light. The critical factor in this intervention is that in order for the Fifth Dimensional frequencies of Limitless Solar Transmutation to be effectively integrated into our present third dimensional experiences on

Earth, they must be consciously drawn through the Heart Flames of Lightworkers abiding on Earth. Otherwise, even though this blessed Light is pouring into the atmosphere on Earth, we will not receive Its miraculous benefits in our daily life. This would be a tragedy beyond our comprehension. Fortunately, a plan has been set into motion by the entire Company of Heaven to avert such a tragedy.

Please go within the Divinity of your own Heart Flame and invoke the Light of Illumined Truth through every fiber of your Being. Read these words carefully, and as you do, ask the Presence of God blazing in your Heart to reveal to you your part in this Divine Plan. Then, respond according to your Inner Heart Call, knowing with full confidence that the doors will open to pave the way for you to fulfill your part of the Plan.

Pulsating in the Etheric Realms over the Southern portion of Mexico, all of the Caribbean Islands, the Dominican Republic and Cuba is a tremendous vortex of the Violet Transmuting Flame. This Forcefield of Divine Light has been building in momentum for thousands of years. It has been sustained by the Solar Archangels of the Seventh Ray of Spiritual Freedom—Beloved Zadkiel and His Divine Complement, Archaii Holy Amethyst.

During past Cosmic Moments on Earth, this vortex has been opened for a brief period of time to allow the Sacred Violet Fire of Transmutation to pour into the physical plane of Earth. This was done with the Divine Intent of establishing a frequency of Freedom on Earth that would lift all Humanity out of our oppressive, humanly created state of fear, pain and suffering into the Illumined Truth of our Divine Heritage as Sons and Daughters of God.

Unfortunately, in the past we were separated from our Holy Christ Self so completely that we experienced very little success from this activity of Transmutation, and the success we did accomplish was very short-lived because the lower human ego would quickly return to its wayward consciousness.

Now, for the first time since the "fall of man" many millenia ago, we are reunited with our Solar Christ Presence. This means that as we learn to integrate this aspect of ourself into our four lower bodies (physical, etheric, mental and emotional), these vehicles will be transformed into the perfection that they were originally supposed to express. Our bodies were originally created to reflect only the perfection of our Holy Christ Self: Eternal Youth, Vibrant Health and Radiant Beauty. When we fell into darkness and separated from our Christ Self, we began to experience all of the maladies we are currently plagued with: aging, disease, death as we know it, poverty, fear, hate, loneliness, unhappiness, etc. We developed the distorted personality of our lower human ego, and over time, we began to accept this sad state of affairs as a normal part of our Earthly experience.

All of that has now been dramatically changed. Being reunited with our Divine Self has opened doors of opportunity we have never dared to dream were possible. We, at long last, actually have the ability to regain our direction and to transform our Earthly life back into the experience of health, loving relationships, a fulfilling job, prosperity, happiness, high self-esteem and all of the other attributes of joy that we have been longing for. But, *and this is the most important fact of all,* we still have free will, and in order to transform our life, we must consciously *choose* to do so, and then take the *necessary steps* to integrate our Solar Christ Presence into our daily life experiences with every thought, word, action and feeling we express.

I know this seems like a monumental task, but we are being given exceptionally powerful assistance from the Realms of Perfection to accomplish this goal.

We are on the dawn of transformation, and the initial impulse of Limitless Physical Perfection is being made available to all those who choose to utilize the Sacred Gift of

Limitless Solar Transmutation.

Beginning with the second Ascension Activity of January 11, 1993, the Violet Transmuting Flame vortex of Archangel Zadkiel and Holy Amethyst began receiving, from the Heart of God, the most intensified frequency of Limitless Solar Transmutation Cosmic Law would allow. It was projected into the consciousness and the Heart Flame of every Lightworker on the Planet. Daily and hourly It built in momentum until It reached a crescendo on the Summer Solstice of June 21, 1993. For seven days this crescendo of Holy Light bathed all life evolving on Earth, giving every man, woman and child, every Elemental and every Angelic Presence abiding on Earth, the opportunity to release ALL of our miserable afflictions, maladies, addictions, obsessions, negative behavior patterns, dysfunctional emotions, painful experiences, limiting conditions, distorted perceptions, erroneous and destructive belief systems, illusions and ignorance. The release of these conditions and states of consciousness cleared the way for our Solar Christ Presence to take full dominion of our four lower bodies.

Once that occurred, this Divine Aspect of ourself began to raise our bodies into their rightful state of Limitless Physical Perfection. Our physical realities, our daily life experiences, will now gradually begin to reflect this perfection, and they will be transformed. Negative experiences such as those being pushed to the surface in our life cannot exist in the presence of Light. This means that, through the Divine Gift of Light, our life can now be restored to Harmony and Balance, Health, Prosperity, Eternal Youth, Joy, Fulfillment, Happiness and Abounding Love.

This may seem too good to be true, but just remember, even though the miracles of God always seem too good to be true, they ARE true, and all we have to do is allow them to manifest in our life to prove it.

This Divine Activity of Light was accomplished through the unified efforts of Lightworkers all over the world. We were asked by the entire Company of Heaven to create an opportunity for those Lightworkers who wanted to respond to this Clarion Call for assistance from on High. We arranged an event that vastly transformed the lives of all those who volunteered to participate. Through the Heart Flames of the selfless volunteers, the Light of Limitless Solar Transmutation was made available for the transformation of all life on Earth. It was imperative that we gather within the Etheric Forcefield of the Violet Flame of Limitless Solar Transmutation in the Caribbean for the seven-day period during which the crescendo of this Holy Light bathed the Planet. We balanced the accelerated purification all life received by harmonizing our emotional bodies. The water element is the predominant substance in our emotional bodies, so we connected deeply with the emotional body (the water element) of Mother Earth during this sacred opportunity.

We were directed to organize this Activity of Light as the Seventh Annual World Congress On Illumination. This Congress carried the full-gathered momentum of the Seventh Ray of Spiritual Freedom, and we joined together for a very, very Spiritual Caribbean Cruise, so that we would actually be on the water within the vortex of Limitless Transmutation.

That World Congress was unique. Each day was a very important time of releasing and completing the blocks and resistance of our past that were preventing us from manifesting the joy and abundance that are our natural birthright as Children of God.

Each morning we had powerful activities of Light that enabled us to take full advantage of the Solar Light of Limitless Transmutation. We also took full advantage of the cruise itself because, as we experienced the fun, joy and laughter of the cruise, our healing process was accelerated. We went on the shore excursions and connected with the Spiritual energies of the sacred islands. There was a lot of time to spend just absorbing and assimilating the Holy Light as we connected with the water and healing energies.

By being in the actual vortex of this Light and absorbing It into our Heart Flame, we experienced the maximum transformation we were capable of receiving according to our individual Divine Plan, and this Light was made tangibly available for the blessing and transformation of the rest of Humanity and all Lifeforms evolving on Earth.

The Light of God is Eternally Victorious, and during this Cosmic Moment on Earth, It is exceedingly so. Not even the Company of Heaven expected the overwhelming success of the unified efforts of Awakened Humanity that occurred over the Summer Solstice in June, 1993. But, succeed we did, and this Sweet Earth and all Her life will never be the same again. We have Ascended into frequencies of the ***Solar Christ Presence of Humanity***, and the CHRIST will never again recede from Earth.

This Divine Activity of Light was multi-faceted, and every Lightworker participated in this glorious event either consciously or subconsciously, according to their inner Heart Call and their wisdom and understanding. Every contribution was critical to the success of the whole, and no Lightworker was any more significant than another. I would like to share with you some of the aspects of this Divine phase of Earth's Rebirth as they have been revealed to me. This is information that you already hold within your Heart Flame. Now we can all revel in the joy of this moment on a conscious level.

As you know, over the past few years, we have successfully moved through several vibrational shifts on the Planet. These shifts have corrected our course and returned our Sweet Earth to the path of Ascension that was Her original destiny. The details of this process have been simply presented in two of my books, *Your Time Is At Hand* and *The Awakening....Eternal Youth, Vibrant Health and Radiant Beauty*, but for clarity, I will very briefly reiterate some of what has taken place that brought us to this Cosmic Moment.

In 1992 we experienced a year of healing. It was a time when the third dimensional plane and all its Elements (Earth, Air, Water, Fire and Ether) were reunited with the Divine energies of the Planetary Christ Presence. The Planetary Christ Presence is an aspect of our consciousness that was originally intended to be the master of our physical vehicles, our mental vehicles, our emotional vehicles and our etheric vehicles. Unfortunately, when Humanity fell from Grace, through the misuse of our creative faculties of thought and feeling, we developed a lower level of consciousness that we refer to as the human ego. This fallen consciousness functions strictly to gratify the physical senses. As it became the predominant influence over our four lower bodies, we experienced a separation, a literal short circuit, that disconnected us from our Planetary Christ Presence. This tragic event created a situation that prevented Humanity from remembering our Divine Origin, and it forced us to look at the limited third dimensional plane as our only reality. Of all the dimensions we abide in simultaneously, the physical plane is the least REAL of all; it is merely a reflection of our consciousness. It is actually referred to as the world of illusion.

After much preparation, in 1992, on the fifth anniversary of Harmonic Convergence (August 17th), Lightworkers created a unified Cup of Consciousness, a Chalice, a Holy Grail, into which the Light of a thousand Suns poured. This created a Bridge of Light and healed the short circuit that disconnected Humanity from our Planetary Christ Presence. This Holy Light physically and tangibly spliced the RNA-DNA patterns of our physical bodies, at an atomic cellular level, to the Divine Blueprint of the RNA-DNA patterns of our Planetary Christ Presence. This Divine activity permanently healed our self-inflicted separation from our Planetary Christ Presence, and it began the process through which our Holy Christ Self will integrate into our cellular structures.

After the Victorious Accomplishment of the return of our Planetary Christ Presence, we were ready for the next phase of our healing. Held within the embrace of the Goddess of Liberty, during the Sun Cycle of Libra (October, 1992), Lightworkers were asked by the Company of Heaven to gather in the Celestial Focus of the Sun which is anchored on the Island of the Sun in Lake Titicaca, Bolivia. During this Holy Conclave, the radiance of our Twelve-fold Solar Spine was infused with the Twelve-fold Solar Causal Body of God. This infusion of Divine Light expanded the ability of every man, woman and child on Earth to project Light into the physical plane a thousand times a thousand-fold. This greatly enhanced the Light of God through every particle of Life on Earth.

This tremendous influx of Light enabled the two remaining "pockets of evil" on the Planet, the regenerating vortexes of the forces of imbalance, to be permanently sealed and Transmuted into Light. These pockets were located in Bolivia and South Africa. After the sealing of these regenerating vortexes of negativity, the forces of imbalance who were trapped in the astral plane of discord that surrounds the Earth were infuriated, fearful and confused. They roamed the psychic-astral plane in a state of panic looking for some door of Humanity's consciousness through which they could again connect with the physical plane. This was an aspect of the time revealed in Revelations when Jesus said these energies (Satan) would be "loosed on the Earth." This increased psychic-astral pressure created an upheaval of emotional turbulence on the Planet and exacerbated Humanity's etheric records of emotional pain, grief and suffering. Eighty percent of our Earthly energies are expressed through our Emotional Bodies, so consequently, as all of the painful experiences of our Earthly existence began to stir and rise to the surface, we started to feel overwhelmed and, at levels, even hopeless. If you will just reflect on what your life was like from October, 1992, to June, 1993, I think you will clearly see the increase in emotional turmoil that occurred. This was individual and global. I don't know a soul who didn't go through some kind of emotional crisis. This ranged from personal doubts and fears about themself to every other kind of emotional challenge—relationships, careers, health, finances, global problems, wars, natural disasters, etc. This also included an increase in uncomfortable feelings that often couldn't even be identified with a current experience. Many people, for no apparent reason, were experiencing increased anger, anxiety, fear, irritability, impatience, panic attacks, depression, despair, grief, sadness, confusion, hopelessness and despondency. This emotional chaos fed the psychic-astral plane, and for a time, it fulfilled the purpose of sustaining the forces of imbalance. It became clear to all of the Powers that Be in the Heavenly Realms that the Earth was in serious trouble.

A Divine Plan was set into motion to counter the emotional turbulence. The Celestial Configurations that influence our Earth were taken into consideration, and a Plan was formed to take full advantage of the currents of Spiritual Energy flowing into the Planet.

THE NEPTUNE/URANUS CONJUNCTION

In 1993, a rare conjunction occurred between the Planets Neptune and Uranus. Neptune has always ruled the Water Element, which is the elemental substance associated with the Emotional Body. Uranus is the Planet in our Solar System most aligned with the Seventh Solar Aspect, the Violet Ray of Transmutation. These Planets conjunct only once every 171 years. This was the first time Humanity was *consciously* aware of these two Heavenly Bodies during a conjunction.

I know, at the present time, there is a great deal of controversy over the validity of astrology, and I agree that currently there is much human conjecture, error, speculation and even superstition involved in the interpretation of it, but it is naive for us not to acknowledge that, as we move from one major forcefield of energy to another, there are bound to be effects and changes on the Earth. All we have to do is observe what takes place when we have a full moon or when a Sunspot flairs up or when a comet passes the Earth or the effects of a Solar or Lunar Eclipse to realize we are *very* affected by every change in the Solar System, especially when we move into the energy field of two Planets as powerful as Neptune and Uranus. These two Planets are powerful in themselves, but their influence was greatly amplified by the rare conjunction. Another factor that empowered this conjunction was 1993's (1+9+9+3=22) 22 vibration. Twenty-two is a Master Number that *greatly accentuates* every single frequency of vibration occurring within its embrace. This amplification is indiscriminate and affects everything in its path regardless of whether it is positive or negative.

Consequently, it was imperative for us to hold the focus of our attention on the positive life transforming goals we wanted to bring into physical manifestation in 1993. We needed to carefully monitor our thoughts, words, actions and feelings that year because "where your attention is, there you are." We had the opportunity of experiencing instant manifestation or "cash karma," which means we witnessed the almost instantaneous return of our energy.

Prior to the "fall" of Humanity, the natural influences of the Heavenly Bodies of our Solar System, which sequentially flow into the Planet Earth as we revolve in our orbit, were always designed to be a blessing. They carry the vibrations of Divinity and were originally supposed to positively enhance our growth and evolution. Unfortunately, when we became immersed in negativity, the incoming Light from the Heavenly Bodies surrounding Earth amplified the negative as well as the positive. As we became aware of this, astrologers began to *warn* Humanity of the coming Planetary influences, and Astrology changed from a Sacred Science of joy and expectation to a prophecy of dread and fear.

Now, the Planet Earth is Ascending into the Light, and the veil of discord and illusion is being Transmuted. Once again we have the opportunity to utilize the Divine Light of the Heavenly Bodies as our Father-Mother God intended in the beginning. When we CONSCIOUSLY participate in these Divine events, they affect each of us immeasurably.

We are now experiencing a new awareness. Our relationship with nature and our environment is changing. We are beginning to revere our physical bodies as the "Temple of the Living God" they were originally intended to be. Our addictions and compulsive behavior patterns are being exposed in the Light of Truth for our Illumination. We are learning what is truly healthy for our precious Earthly vehicles, and our God Self is once again taking dominion to implement the Laws of Health.

Uranus is the Planet of insight, awareness and illumination. Neptune balances the water element and brings harmony to the emotional body. Neptune also brings new ideals and new levels of faith and accomplishment. The union of these two Mighty Forces created an environment that allowed great change and personal transformation. We have the ability to utilize the building momentum of energy that was anchored during the Neptune/Uranus conjunction to empower our Spiritual, emotional and physical healing. This energy has been permanently anchored on Earth through the Heart Flames of all Lightworkers.

Each day it is vitally important for us to positively direct this immense planetary force of Light. In gratitude, we must focus on our personal vision of transformation. Write a detailed description of your goals, dreams and aspirations. See them physically manifest here and now. Affirm them in the present time as though they already exist in this Cosmic Moment, the Eternal Moment of Now. Affirm your Eternal Youth, Vibrant Health, Radiant Beauty, Limitless Prosperity, Fulfilling Job, Loving Relationships, Spiritual Freedom, Oneness with God, Joy, Happiness and every other Divine Quality, Attribute and Experience. Expand your vision of Heaven on Earth to include every man, woman and child, every Elemental and Being of the Nature Kingdom, every particle of life evolving on Earth. In your mind's eye, tenaciously hold the vision of this Blessed Planet adorned in Her Seamless Garment of Light, pulsating in Her resplendent beauty and harmony. Remember always, the purpose and reason for your being on Earth is to learn to use your creative faculties of thought and feeling to become the master of energy, vibration and consciousness. You are to be a co-Creator with God, and never before have you had a greater opportunity to fulfill this Divine Mission.

1993 was a "moment" when major planetary cycles were profoundly aligned. This created a transition of Global consciousness that liberated us from the "old world" of limitation and illusion. The "New World" consciousness of Limitless Physical Perfection and Reverence for all Life is now being projected as a Divine Blueprint on the atomic cellular structures of all manifest form. This activity enables us to lift beyond the lower human ego consciousness. It creates a window of opportunity which empowers us to connect with the multi-dimensional aspects of our true God Reality. This Divine Self gratefully moves us beyond the limitation of our human ego boundaries. Through this reunion, we will open to greater Enlightenment realizing levels of human potential we have long forgotten.

The Neptune/Uranus Conjunction created a frequency of independence and human dignity. Leaders and governments began to experience this Divine Light, and they responded according to their wisdom and understanding. Lightworkers now have the ability *and* the responsibility of holding the Immaculate Concept for the unfoldment of the Divine Plan for all world governments. We don't have to figure out the logistics for each government; we just need to invoke the God Presence of everyone involved and ask that only the Divine Plan manifest through him/her according to the highest good for all concerned. Through each one, change will occur, supporting the growing vision for Heaven on Earth.

The exact conjunction of Neptune and Uranus throughout 1993 represented the actual birth of a new consciousness of Global Oneness. We now have the opportunity to experience new visions, new breakthroughs and new ways of living. Our personal responsibility for Global conditions has been awakened within us, and there is no turning back. Together we shall, God Victoriously, participate in creating a New World.

As we progressed into 1993, all Humanity experienced an amplified wake-up call that alerted us to even greater awareness and responsibility. It will be difficult for us to continue in denial. Personal and social issues that do not express a Reverence for all Life must be addressed. This was a major turning point in which our direction and our purpose were renewed. We will now be able to move beyond limiting circumstances, if we will only hold our attention on our vision and accept our new reality.

Our experiences of the past can be healed and, at long last, we are free to move toward the joy and fulfillment we have been longing for in our life.

This is a time to "WALK OUR TALK." Stay in truth. Focus on our vision. And above all, experience laughter and joy.

HEALING OUR EMOTIONAL BODIES

With the empowerment of the Neptune/Uranus Conjunction, the Divine Plan was set into motion through the unified efforts of the entire Company of Heaven and Awakened Humanity. Fifth Dimensional frequencies of the Violet Flame of LIMITLESS Transmutation were projected into the emotional stratum of Earth and into the Emotional Bodies of every Human Being evolving on Earth, whether they were in or out of embodiment. The purpose was for the discordant emotional frequencies of pain and suffering back to the "fall" of Humanity aeons ago to be pushed to the surface and bathed in the Violet Flame of Limitless Transmutation, thus purging and Transmuting the emotional pain of the Ages—cause, core, effect, record and memory.

Our Emotional Bodies have recorded within them every feeling we have ever experienced since we were first breathed forth from the Heart of God. Since the "fall," most of our feelings have reflected the fear and pain of the lower human ego. Consequently, the great majority of the energy stored in our Emotional Bodies is qualified with frequencies of seemingly unbearable grief and fear. The Emotional Body of Mother Earth, the Water Element, is also seething with the accumulation of Humanity's pain and the pain we have inflicted upon the Elemental Kingdom and the environment of Earth as well. As long as we remained submerged in this sea of emotional grief, we very effectively nourished the psychic-astral realms of chaos. This perpetuated our vicious circle of suffering. The more pain we were in, the more susceptible we were to the influence of this realm of deception and the more influence the psychic-astral realm had over us, the further we fell away from the realization of our own Divinity. This created a victim consciousness that made us feel helpless and hopeless. This dysfunctional scenario has been the order of the day on Earth for quite some time. But now, in order for the Christ to again be in command, it must cease.

Beginning with the influx of the Winter Solstice on December 21, 1992, the Divine Plan for the Transmutation of our Emotional Bodies was set into motion. The Goddess of Liberty, the Divine Exponent of the Seventh Solar Aspect of Liberation, agreed to accept the responsibility of enfolding this Sweet Earth in Her Luminous Presence. She expanded Her Heart Flame to envelop the entire Planet in an unprecedented Forcefield of the Violet Flame of Liberation to assist in the Plan of Liberating the Planet and Humanity from the emotional pain and suffering of the past. We then moved into the frequencies of the New Year.

Additional assistance was granted from on High as the entire Universe focused its attention on this small, fallen Planet. Never before has a Planet this contaminated been given the opportunity to move into the Light so quickly. It is a unique experiment that is being observed by all life from the very Core of Creation.

The Violet Transmuting Flame vortex of Archangel Zadkiel and Holy Amethyst began receiving the most intensified frequency of Limitless Solar Transmutation from the very Heart of God that Cosmic Law would allow. It was projected into the consciousness and the Heart Flame of every Lightworker on the Planet. Daily and hourly It built in momentum until It reached a crescendo on the Summer Solstice on June 21, 1993. For seven days this crescendo of Holy Light bathed all life evolving on Earth giving every man, woman and child, every Elemental and every Angelic Presence abiding on Earth the opportunity to release ALL of our miserable emotions and behavior patterns. The release of these conditions and states of consciousness cleared the way for our Solar Christ Presence to take full dominion of our four lower bodies.

During the seven-day period in which the crescendo of this Holy Light bathed the Planet, we balanced the accelerated purification all life was receiving by harmonizing our Emotional Bodies. The water element is the predominant substance in our Emotional Bodies, so it was necessary to connect deeply with the Emotional Body (the water element) of Mother Earth during this sacred opportunity.

Two hundred Awakened souls joined us physically on the cruise, and thousands joined us in consciousness from their Forcefields of Light around the Globe. In addition to those who were consciously participating in this Divine Plan, the Holy Christ Self of every man, woman and child joined with us at Inner Levels, and the entire Elemental Kingdom and Angelic Kingdom serving the Earth at this time also joined with us in consciousness.

On the Full Moon of June 20, 1993, the gathering of Lightworkers began in Florida. Beloved Lunara, the Feminine Director of the Water Element and the Divine Complement of Neptune, the Masculine Director of the Water Element, began to flood the oceans, seas, lakes, rivers, springs, creeks, water ways and every molecule of water on Earth with the Solar Radiance of a New Order of Healing. The Emerald Green Solar Ray of Healing with a Violet radiance of Limitless Transmutation poured into the waters of Earth preparing every electron of emotional energy to receive the most Powerful Healing allowed by Cosmic Law. Archangel Zadkiel and Holy Amethyst stood in readiness, and as the first Rays of Sunlight burst through the darkness heralding the first impulse of the Summer Solstice (June 21, 1993), our Father-Mother God began magnetizing from the very core of Creation, the most intensified activity of the Violet Flame of Limitless Transmutation the Earth could withstand. The entire Company of Heaven joined with Archangel Zadkiel and Holy Amethyst, and as One Breath, One Heartbeat, One Consciousness of Pure Divine Love, the Fifth Dimensional Light of the Violet Flame of Limitless Transmutation was breathed into the Heart Flames of the embodied Lightworkers on Earth. This unification of Heaven and Earth created a PERMANENT OPEN PORTAL between the two realms, through which this Divine Light will continually pour until all life on this Sweet Earth is wholly Ascended and Free.

This Activity of Light began the seven day purging of the Emotional Strata and Emotional Bodies of Humanity.

TRANSMUTATION OF THE ANTI-CHRIST ENERGIES

After the first few days of Transmutation and Healing, it was revealed to the Lightworkers that the next phase of the Divine Plan was going to be attempted. Preparation for this phase of the plan began several years ago in Medjugorje, Yugoslavia. Mother Mary revealed to us that within the vortex of Yugoslavia are great forces of Light and great forces of darkness, both in and out of embodiment, who have volunteered to create the pageant that would escort the miscreations of Humanity, often called the anti-Christ energies, into the higher schools of learning. Mother Mary said in order to prepare for this Cosmic Moment, She projected Her Luminous Presence into the Forcefield of Yugoslavia (Medjugorje) for several years. Hundreds of thousands of souls from all over the world were drawn into Yugoslavia by Her Presence. As the souls came on their Holy Pilgimages, they brought Rays of Light from their homelands and anchored them into Yugoslavia. Then a Ray of Divine Light from Yugoslavia was anchored in their Heart Flames and carried back to their homelands on their return journey. This created myriad highways of Light from all over the World into Yugoslavia.

The war occurring now in Yugoslavia is symbolically representing the progressive descent of the lower human ego into chaos and hatred. Yugoslavia is representing a microcosm of the macrocosm. When the oppressive yoke of Communism was removed from Yugoslavia, instead of reveling in the joy of their newfound freedom, the lower human ego activated ancient hatreds. This caused men to pick up arms, as they began a systematic slaughter through "ethnic cleansing." This consciousness is typical of the depravity of the human ego, and it is the epitome of the consciousness referred to as the anti-Christ.

The anti-Christ is, in reality, any frequency of vibration or any level of consciousness that conflicts with the perfection of the Christ. It is not specifically one entity or devil, but rather the accumulation of all of Humanity's misqualified thoughts, words, actions and feelings. It is hate, pain, poverty, disease, suffering, fear, oppression, limitation, separation and all other aspects of existence that do not reflect the Harmony, Balance, Love and Oneness of God. It is the confusion and pandemonium of the psychic-astral plane and the discarnate souls who are trapped there perpetuating the chaos and fear. It is our lower human ego with all of its treachery, and IT IS TIME FOR THE ANTI-CHRIST TO BE BANISHED FROM THE EARTH!!!

This was indeed the next phase of the Plan. A representative from Croatia (formerly Yugoslavia) was sponsored by Lightworkers to come on the Spiritual Cruise and be physically in the vortex of Limitless Transmutation. In Croatia, Lightworkers were prepared to receive the Violet Light of Limitless Transmutation. Through a Divine Ceremony, the Light of God that is always Victorious was projected through the Silent Watcher of Croatia (see illustration pages 43 and 44) into the Heart Flames of the Lightworkers there and through them INTO EVERY FREQUENCY OF ANTI-CHRIST ENERGY SYMBOLICALLY MANIFESTING IN CROATIA AND THROUGHOUT *ALL* OF FORMER YUGOSLAVIA TO ALL MANIFESTATIONS OF THE ANTI-CHRIST ON EARTH.

This merciful activity of God's Light created an opening in the psychic-astral plane that allowed the souls trapped there to be freed into the Inner Schools of Learning if they chose to move forward in the Light.

This literally freed millions of fallen souls who had been trapped for hundreds of thousands of years in this realm of human miscreation. This activity of Light also cut us free from the immobilizing grip of our lower human ego which has, up until this time, blocked the integration of the Holy Christ Self into our four lower bodies.

This purging of the anti-Christ was accomplished in perfect Divine Order in the *Realms of Cause.* Now, we will gradually begin to experience the incredible freedom of that gift as it begins to reflect in the physical *World of Effects.* This will be a process, but we should feel a lifting of the oppressive interference of the psychic-astral plane IMMEDIATELY.

I would like to share with you a letter we received from our friend from Croatia after his experience on the Spiritual Cruise at the Seventh Annual World Congress on Illumination.

Dearest Patti and Kay:

To be with you and with so many wonderful souls was really a marvelous experience.

Thank you for the extraordinary events that happened during the Congress. So great was the inflow of the Transmuting Energy of the Violet Flame that all were purified to a very high degree. If some were not visibly purified to the surface of their human dimension, nevertheless the Energy which persists in them is powerful and will continue to Transmute them, to change them anyway.

Many will need a little time to experience fully **what** happened there at the Congress. Changes will manifest little by little. But they have **accepted** the change into themselves. Even more, it is not important if they believe or not, the change will come out anyway. Of course, it will be sooner or immediate if it is recognized in full awareness.

I believe that you remember the Words in God's Message given to me during the cruise: "I invited you to will stress the words "**more** of My Life," and "**more** of My Light." Yes, **that** was what happened there, what happened to every participant already. I was so full of Energy, of His Life, Light and Love, that it was even difficult to bear it. The whole life that I am was and is so tremendously widened and powerful in its radiation that it is almost at the edge of possibility to stay in human form. God's Presence in me is making the change perfect. Really, **more** of His Life, **more** of His Light began to express through me than before coming to the Congress. The great Violet Light Transmuted my structure in such a way that tremendous Light Energy is radiating through my appearance.

Oh, how powerful is His Light in me, how powerful is His Love in me! I AM Light, I AM Love. As a Blazing Amethyst I AM.

I just got a lovely letter from a dear friend. She heard about my coming to the Congress, and she is expecting changes in me in the next few months. She remembers her own experiences during her attendance at the first World Congress On Illumination in Hawaii, when Archangel Uriel began to speak to her. She remembers her changes, and she knows my innerness very, very well, just as others could see my innerness. So, the changes are present, and changes we can expect.

The participants of the World Congress On Illumination **have** new experiences, are experiencing the deep change in themselves. If some of them do not have such experiences, they have just to wait with patience and believe, because the change will come. Everyone of them is going through deep, deep change.

Do you not feel yourself purified, filled to the fullness with His Life, His Love, His Light, Peace and Freedom? Try to see yourselves, dear participants of the Congress, in your stillness, and you will see that you are less in human limitations, that your Divinity is coming out, purifying you so that you become "transparent," so to speak, and your Divinity has only TO BE through you.

See yourself as a Blazing Amethyst, Transmuted into the Divine Being, and you will experience such Freedom that will nevermore close itself for you. YOU **ARE** REBORN. The Vortex of the Transmuting Violet Flame went through you and is continuing to affect you so powerfully that your change is certain. It already happened. Just wait for it, and it will reveal itself to you as your new life, as your Perfect Life. Nothing is left in you of your old life. You are freed. Concentrate yourself to this fact, and YOU WILL SEE IT IN YOURSELF. You will experience your Divinity as yourself alone! Is it not marvelous? This is the time TO BE what you really ARE. There will be no other time; the right time is NOW. And that what I am speaking about is happening to you NOW. It will be not in some future time.

Again and again, I will express my deepest gratitude to Patti and Kay and to all those beautiful souls who made it possible for me to come and attend the World Congress on Illumination. It was **really** Illumination, Illumination for all Humanity, for all Earth.

Please, I send my deepest Love to my dearest friends, to all who surround you, dearest Patti and Kay. I send my deepest Love to all beautiful souls who bear in themselves the new coming of God into the world, who are rebirthing Him onto Earth, who are making that Heaven descend onto the Earth - to those souls that I met at the Congress and to those around the world that are the same as we are, Blessed with the Light and Love of God, and I AM in them as Love, as Light and as Life because I AM that I AM.

I would like to express my deepest gratitude that I was able to come and share with all of you this unique moment of time, to be a part of it. And I express my very special gratitude to all of you who supported my coming with your love offerings. The same gratefulness I am sending to all those who sent their love offerings although it was impossible for them to be there. And my thanks to those beautiful souls who supported my coming with their love.

Above all, thank you for this special meeting for Croatia. I know that Croatian people will be deeply grateful and will appreciate all you do for peace in my country.

Let me include a brief prayer:

Thank you God for this opportunity to share with these beautiful souls Your Love, Your Light, Your Peace, Your Almighty Presence.

In this most significant time of human history, Lightworkers have descended from on High to anchor the Transmuting energy of the Violet Flame. Some of them were trained and were descended to bring Transmuting Energy to the regions where peace prevails. They are the **Workers of Light** because they come to the peaceful parts of the world and nothing opposes them. They can work in peace. But there are regions where darkness is so dense and so horribly destructive that specially trained Lightworkers are needed. They are the **Warriors of Light.**

The territory of Croatia is one of such places. That what is happening here is a result of the process of purification, during which many souls will depart from this plane because of very special purposes. Therefore, the Lightworkers or spiritual leaders in Croatia are specially trained for this crucial moment of the world, appearing many times on the Earth, always going through the most difficult social situations in the history of the world. They learned the horror of condensed negative energies, and they know **how** to oppose it.

The darkness of negative energies there is so dense, destructing through the aggressors, that even the wise cannot see. Although the majority of Lightworkers in Croatia were born under the constant influence of the Violet Light, so that they are really "The Blazing Amethysts" of our beautiful country, and although they are well-trained and prepared for the battle with negative energies, they couldn't accomplish their task without direct intervention of God Himself. God reveals Himself to some of them, guiding them directly or even manifesting through them some of His Perfect Attributes. In this way, they can fight against the negativity, not only with God's Light and Love, but as His Almighty I AM Presence. They are out of the destructive energies. They are fully protected.

There are great Light and Love activities in Croatia, and Zagreb, its capital, is a very strong center of Light here.

A few years ago I founded, in Zagreb, the New Age Centre, named also Community of God's Light and Love. We are working fundamentally with the teachings of St. Germain, Group Avatar, and The New Age Study of Humanity's Purpose. Before this terrible warfare, we have published our magazine "Revelations," but now we had to stop because of the deep economic crisis.

And I will finish with one message given to me during our cruise. When Patti said yesterday, "Write down onto your violet paper whatever comes from your Heart," this message came out:

"My dear child, you are one with Me. Don't be afraid. I have promised you I will come soon, so I Am coming to you. Did I not promise that I will reveal Myself to you, My Beloved? Be in peace. I Am with you, I AM you, as you know already.

"I invited you to come here to give you even more of My Life, to give you more of My Light, to be completely One with you.

"Bring My Light to all because you are All, because I AM All. And I AM always with you."

Thank you,
D. G.

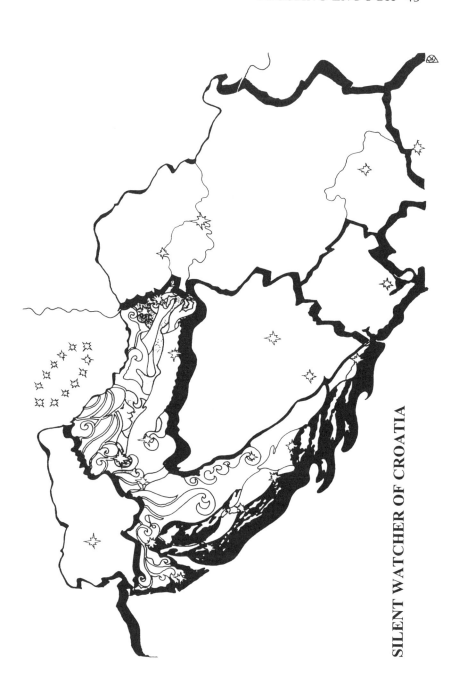

SILENT WATCHER OF CROATIA

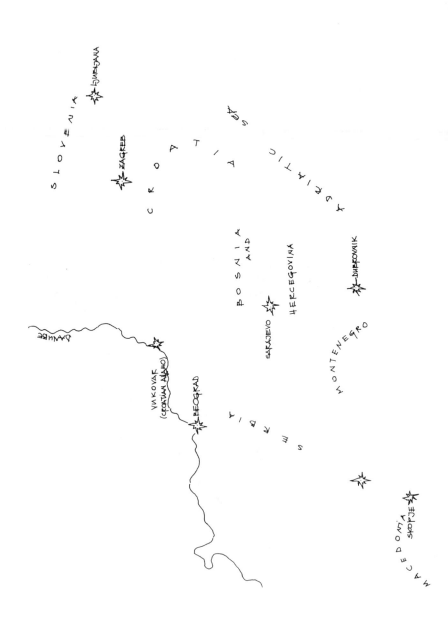

Not even the Company of Heaven knew how much of the anti-Christ energies would be removed. Everything is always contingent on Humanity's clarity and free will. We were told the success of this Activity of Light far exceeded even the greatest expectations of Heaven. The joy and elation pouring forth from the Realms of Perfection were overwhelming.

The successful removal of the *majority of* anti-Christ energies enabled our Father-Mother God to implement the next phase of Earth's Ascension in the Light far ahead of schedule.

The next glorious Activity of Light took place on June 26, 1993. On this Holy Day, after the Violet Flame of Limitless Transmutation had successfully purged the discordant emotional energies of Humanity's pain and suffering from the Planet in the Realms of Cause and the anti-Christ energies had been predominently Transmuted, and hundreds of thousands of trapped souls freed into the Inner Schools of Learning, a window of opportunity opened that allowed the SOLAR CHRIST PRESENCE OF HUMANITY TO RETURN TO EARTH. For aeons of time, the oppressive lower human ego and anti-Christ energies had effectively blocked the RETURN OF THE CHRIST. Now, with these energies greatly dissipated, nothing was standing in the way of the Christ. The Cosmic Edict rang forth from the Heart of God, and in one Mighty Stroke, the **SOLAR CHRIST PRESENCE RETURNED TO EARTH.**

This is truly the fulfillment of the Second Coming of the Christ. Each and every Lifestream evolving on Earth is now reunited with the Solar Aspect of their Holy Christ Presence. This is the part of our Being that reflects the true Son or Daughter of God we actually are. This is the ultimate realization of our own Divinity.

It is difficult for us to grasp the magnitude of just what this means, but this is the reunification with our Divinity, and it has assured the transformation of our physical reality into Heaven on Earth. Again, this was Victoriously Accomplished in the Realms of Cause, and now, as we focus on this Divine Aspect of ourself, It will gradually reflect into our daily life manifesting Heaven on Earth and Limitless Physical Perfection.

For the first time, we are reunited with our Solar Christ Presence. As we learn to integrate this Presence of Light through our four lower bodies (physical, etheric, mental and emotional), these vehicles will be transformed into the perfection that they were originally supposed to express.

Being reunited with our Divine Self has opened doors of opportunity we have never dared to dream were possible. And it is critical that we take the *necessary steps* to integrate our Solar Christ Presence into our daily life experiences with every thought, word, action and feeling we express.

One of the most important changes that has taken place since the return of our Solar Christ Presence is that *this Divine Presence encapsulates the Light of God in an invincible armor of Love **before** It enters our four lower vehicles.* This prevents any of the contamination of the lower vehicles from changing the vibration, color or sound of God's Divine Light. Prior to the return of the Solar Christ Presence, all Light passing through us was subject to the feelings we were experiencing at the time. If we were angry or fearful, even the most Holy Light picked up the vibrations of anger or fear as It passed through us and was distorted to a degree. Because of this phenomenon, our God Presence would withhold the Divine Light passing through us until we were in a state of harmony again. This greatly limited our ability to be powerful Lightworkers. We were ineffective unless we were centered and harmonious. Now, even if we are off-center due to our daily challenges, we can still invoke the Light of God and expect the full force of Its Perfection to flow into the situation at hand. This will greatly assist us in quickly clearing and Transmuting the negativity in our personal life and on Earth. It will enable us to be powerful forces of Light even in the face of our human frailties, until our Solar Christ Presence is in full command of our every thought, word, action and feeling, once and for all.

THE OPEN PORTAL
OF THE VIOLET FLAME OF
LIMITLESS TRANSMUTATION

(The following is reprinted with permission from Group Avatar)

Radiation, Vibration and Consciousness from the Spirit of Transformation:

The Violet Fire is "the lead Ray" for this Cosmic Moment on Earth. I come to Earth along Its Spiritual River of Freedom, of which Transformation and Invocation play an integral role...as do Transmutation, Forgiveness, Hope and Liberation. It is all part of the **Mother God reasserting Her Sacred Self with Cosmic Power** on the physical realm of Earth through Her Children, the Arisen Christ. The Violet Fire can be seen now with a Pure White Light core, within which is a Three-fold Flame. Through the Violet Fire now comes the One Great Light of the Universal "I Am", which is everything necessary for the Transformation of this Sweet Star of Freedom. **The Violet Fire Itself is a Forcefield of Solar Light** with all the Twelve Rays of the Father-Mother God functioning under Its influence. This is the principal Cause in Action at this Cosmic Moment, representing as It does, the Perfect Balance of the Masculine and Feminine Aspects of Deity. It is God's Love and God's Power united in newfound God Illumination on Earth, the Arisen Christ! It is bringing Transformation and taking Humanity through Her Ascension! This Sacred Violet Fire is the Keynote of your present embodiment, whichever Ray is your principal Spiritual Avocation. Contemplate Its fullness as It pours through your life.

The tangible goal during this present Cycle of Transformation is a profound **Hope** Resurrecting deep within Humanity, re-uniting the outer consciousness with the Christ "I Am" Consciousness now expanding at the center of every human being. Transformation will bring a Celestial sense of Liberation, tangibly Illuminating the outer consciousness to the Divinity in every other aspect of life around it. Feel with the full Cosmic Forcefield of Expectancy! This shall bring a true Reverence and a complete understanding that **all** is but a part of God...One Breath, One Body, One Heart, One Mind, One Consciousness. This Hope, Liberation and Reverence for all Life is the Higher Order Reality that Humanity enters at this time. Know with Cosmic Conviction that you, Humanity, the Cosmic Christ returned to Earth, are this truth made manifest for all life evolving here.

CONFIRMATION FROM NOSTRADAMUS?

The Company of Heaven is always, delightfully, giving us outer world confirmation of our humble efforts to encourage us to keep on keeping on.

When I returned from the Seventh Annual World Congress on Illumination, our Spiritual Cruise, there was a new book waiting in my mail. The book had not been released yet, but its author sent me an advance copy for review. When I picked the book up, it fell open to the page that contained the following information.

(The following is a quote, reprinted with permission, from the new book *NOSTRADAMUS NOW* by Joseph Robert Hochmans. This book is available through:

Sun Publishing Company
P.O. Box 5588
Santa Fe, NM 87502-5588

This is an authoritative interpretation based on Nostradamus' original text.)

IS A PLANETARY INTER-DIMENSION DOORWAY ABOUT TO BE OPENED?

ORIGINAL TEXT:

Loin pres de l'Urne le malin tourne arriere,
Qu'au grand Mars feu donnera empechement:
Vers l'Aquilon au midi la grande fiere,
FLORA tiendra la porte en pensement.

LINE ONE:

Loin pres de l'Urne le malin tourne arriere - "Far near the Urn the wicked one turns back." What we have here are the makings

of an astrological configuration: The "Urn" is the sign of
Aquarius, and in ancient symbology, the "wicked one" was
considered to be the constrictive Planet of Saturn. That it "turns
back" indicates it is in retrograde motion. The opening phrase
"far near" was a cryptic usually employed by the prophet to
designate more than one configuration, or more specifically, to
pinpoint events which would take place between two configurations. In this case, whenever Saturn enters the sign of
Aquarius (or any other sign), its slow motion allows time for at
least two periods of retrograde motion, on the average, during its
passage. It would appear that Nostradamus was designating a
particular inter-retrograde era for the next line's further astrological alignment.

LINE TWO:

Qu'au grand Mars feu donnera empechement - "That to great
Mars fire will give hindrance." If we sweep away the obscurities,
what the seer was actually saying is that the Planet Mars is to be
found in the fire sign of Leo, which would be in opposition to the
configuration of Saturn retrograde in Aquarius above. Yet,
coordinating this with the information there, Nostradamus did
not describe the Mars in Leo opposition as taking place at the
same moment as the retrogrades but when they would be "far and
near," on either side. These are very specific particulars, for in
most cases, because Mars is relatively fast-moving compared
with Saturn, during a Saturnian retrograde, the red planet is most
often found either nearly conjuncted or opposed to Saturn. To
find Mars in Leo exactly between two Saturn retrogrades and in
the sign of Aquarius, is a rarity among configurations. And this
is true even if one calculates these positionings for either a
Babylonian, an Astronomical or an Aquarian shifting of the
signs to compensate for the Procession of the Equinoxes. As
examples, no such configuration took place during Saturn's last
passage through Aquarius (or Capricorn and Sagittarius) in the

1928 to 1934 era; nor will it work with the upcoming 2016-2022, the 2045-2051 or the 2075-2082 eras to manifest in the next century. However, we happen to be in a similar era as of this writing, 1986-1993. So far, in the shiftings for the Aquarian and the Astronomical charts, nothing has come about. But for the upcoming Babylonian chart, there is a definite hit. From May 28 to October 16, 1992, Saturn is retrograde in Aquarius and will be again July 1 to October 28, 1993. In between the two, free of any overlap with either one or the other periods, Mars will be in Leo April 28 to June 23, 1993. Whatever events the prophet forecast in the rest of this verse, there is a good chance it will happen during this designated time—between Easter and the Summer Solstice, 1993.

LINE THREE:

Vers l'Aquilon au midi la grande fiere - "Toward Aquilon to the south the great woman of pride (will come)." The name "Aquilon," as we have already seen in previous studies, is derived from Aquila the Eagle, the uranology constellation which falls across what is now the United States of America and is its chief symbol. "To the south" designates a more specific area, namely the southern portion of the nation, today recognized as stretching from Virginia across the sunnier latitudes all the way to Texas. The wording "toward Aquilon" and "to the south" implies the arrival of something or someone from somewhere else, that this will be the intended destination of travel. Who the subject is, the prophet identified as *la grand fiere*, the great Woman, with the added connotation of someone proud, dignified, possessing finesse; also considered as one held most precious, one who is relied upon for sustenance and guidance. There is, too, the meaning of one who is "haughty," high-minded, regal; likewise *fiere* is related to our words "fierce, fiery," offering us a picture of someone energetic and most singular in the fulfillment of their purpose.

These characteristics are very similar to how Nostradamus described other feminine figures in other verses: the "Woman of the Holy Earth" (IV, 24), the great "Mother" (V, 73), the "Joyous Maid of Bright Splendor" (X, 84), the "Crone Who Moves Slowly" (V, 36), "She Who Offers Honey as a Gift of Love" (Sixain 18), the "great Artemis" (IX, 74) and the "Celestial Muse" (X, 50). In the context in which many of these titles are found, it is clear the prophet was not referring to any ordinary female of human offspring, but was alluding to major feminine archetypes, Goddess figures, who represent the various creative aspects within all beingness. In particular, esoterically, the seer was honoring the World Mother of Humanity, the Earth Mother of the Planet and the Cosmic Mother of the Stars. There is also a fourth Mother not often included with the other three, because She is feared more than the rest, yet plays as important a role as the others in the creation process. She is the Hidden Mother, who brings all things into completion. Her names are many: Kali, Hecate, Sekhmet, Pele, Tiamat, Kybele, the Black Tara, the Black Madonna. It is She who sweeps away so that new growth can occur, a necessary part of our reality, as fall and winter are a necessary part of the cycle of the seasons, as is spring and summer. Because of Humanity's sometimes stubborn resistance to change, it is the Hidden Mother who must often appear as an angry "fierce, fiery" Goddess, the Warrior and Destroyer. However, when Her message is listened to and Humanity lets go of its outmoded ways of thinking and feeling that it has outgrown, it is She who, as the benign "sustainer," can offer a gift most "precious"—the next step in Humanity's evolution and spiritual Initiation. And it is only through Her recognition and *Her inherent power of Transmutation* that She can eventually fuse with the other Three Mothers, in order to bring into manifestation the Fifth Mother, the All Mother, the ultimate expression of Oneness and Totality.

What Nostradamus appears to be predicting here is that some form of expression and energy of the Hidden Mother (and ultimately the All Mother) is going to be influxed into the southern region of America, beginning in 1993.

(Note inserted: Is this referring to the Violet Flame of Limitless Transmutation which is "The Mother God reasserting Her Sacred Self with Cosmic Power"?)

LINE FOUR:

FLORA tiendra la porte en pensement - "FLORA (they) will hold the door (or gateway) in thought." Because the word FLORA is capitalized in the text, it is recognized as being a special name or title. Most commentators are too quick to associate FLORA with the city of Florence in Italy, even though it has nothing to do with the verse's other geographical specifics, "Aquilon" or Aquila - America. The one appellation that contains FLORA that stands out most prominently in the south part of America is "Florida," a perfect syncope. Though today the name Florida has been assigned to that of the famed peninsular state, originally it designated a much larger area. On the maps of Nostradamus' time, a century before the British colonization began, the Spanish used the label "Florida" to cover the entire southeast area of the North American continent—precisely in the same location considered the South today. So FLORA was simply employed as a confirmation for the geographics given in line three.

"They will hold the doorway in thought." Who "they" are understood to be is not clear, though the inference is these are people who are in some way associated with the "great Woman of pride" in line two, who are to prepare for the coming of Her Presence and serve as the catalysts for Her energies. The word *tiendra* can mean not only to "hold" something, but also to preserve and maintain it, suggesting that "they" will be permanent "keepers" and "protectors" of a certain location or locations. What that location/locations will have is a "door," or a "gateway," an entrance or portal into somewhere else. This will not be an ordinary physical opening (though something of a physical nature may exist to anchor it in), for it is to be "held in thought." The word used in the Old French is *pensement,* thought, pensive air, to concentrate, to focus on, mental single-mindedness and clarity; also, something visualized and imaged, then brought to mind and meditated upon again and again. What may be hinted at is some form of etheric inter-dimensional doorway, which will appear only within a physical anchoring structure or configuration and which can only be opened and closed through a concentrated collective visualization technique. The word *pensement* can also have the Latin connotation of "to empower."

THE PROPHECY:

During the very specific "window" time period of April 28 to June 23, 1993, a special group of individuals, if they choose to do so, could create a sacred space or spaces at pre-arranged locations throughout the South in the ancient region of "Florida" that could serve as an etheric doorway opening through which to invite the Hidden and other Mothers (comprising the All Mother), for Her to dwell and manifest Her powers and potential gifts to the world. In terms of the present ongoing evolution of the Earth's new Crystal energy grid system, this is very likely the beginning process of the anchoring in of the Capricorn Node Point, which will be entering into this precise same area in 1996.

THE WELLSPRING OF ETERNAL HOPE

When we observe the negativity surfacing in our individual lives and witness the painful occurrences of war, disease, poverty, homelessness, environmental pollution, floods, famines, destructive weather conditions, dysfunctional families, crime, violence, corruption, drug abuse, prejudice, hate, joblessness, stress, frustration, despondency and total despair, it is very difficult for us to hold onto the belief and inner knowing that we are, in truth, co-creating Heaven on Earth. But, nevertheless, THAT IS EXACTLY WHAT WE ARE DOING! Nobody said it was going to be easy. Nobody even said it was going to be painless. What we have been told, however, by the Realms of Illumined Truth and the Divine Mind of God, is that Heaven on Earth is now not only a viable possibility, but an absolutely ASSURED GOD VICTORIOUS REALITY.

Just think, from the Realms of Perfection we are being told that Heaven on Earth has already been Victoriously accomplished in the Divine Realms of Cause. Now, all we have to do is hold the vision in our consciousness and through our thoughts, words, actions and feelings, magnetize that perfection into the world of form, thus Transfiguring this Sweet Earth into Her Original Divine Birthright...*Freedom's Holy Star.*

I know that seems like a pretty lofty aspiration, but that is exactly why you and I are here on Earth during this unprecedented Cosmic Moment. And, if we weren't capable of pulling this off, we wouldn't have been allowed to embody on Earth at this time. It's that simple.

So, instead of wringing our hands and bemoaning the challenges in our life, we need to reach up in consciousness and tap the Wisdom and Enlightenment that will set us *Free.*

This is such a special time, and we are beginning to get intuitive, inner glimpses of the magnitude of this Cosmic Moment on Earth. People are constantly expressing to me that they are experiencing a "feeling" or a new "level of understanding" about what's happening on Earth and in their life that they were never aware of before. They just seem to "know" things that confused and baffled them in the past. They say their ability to discern what resonates as truth in their Heart is much more obvious, and they have greater clarity and are able to pierce through the veil of illusion to perceive the reality of a situation much more easily. This isn't a skill that they are specifically working toward developing; it just seems to be mysteriously happening.

Even though people are still dealing with the dysfunctional belief systems of low self-esteem, failure and poverty consciousness, worthlessness, abandonment, separation, loneliness, etc., in the midst of the pain and suffering, they are beginning to get brief flashes of absolutely "knowing" that they are truly Sons and Daughters of God, and "all that the Father has is mine." Even though they are feeling overwhelmed by the enormity of the challenges manifesting on the Planet and sometimes helpless in their ability to change things, they keep hearing an inner voice that repeats again and again, *"You came to Love this Sweet Earth and all Her life free, and all the skills and knowledge you need to accomplish your goal are already within you."* When a person is feeling worthless and helpless, that statement seems rather ludicrous, but there is a new *"inner knowing"* that, for a brief glimmer of time, allows one to accept that truth as unequivocally real.

It is a true paradox that one minute we are feeling like worthless "worms in the dust," and the next minute we *know* that we are Sons and Daughters of God. But, there is a logical explanation as to why this phenomenon is occurring with ever-increasing frequency at this time. Since the return of the Solar Christ Presence, we have been undergoing a Transformational Healing that is reconnecting us with the Realms of Illumined Truth and Knowledge. It was never part of the original Divine Plan that we be separated from this Realm but, due to our curiosity and the misuse of our creative faculties of thought and feeling, we manifested this situation.

For aeons of time, we have mistakenly been accepting this third dimensional reality as the only reality, and we have believed that our physical body is who we are. Imagine, we have been accepting only a minuscule part of our true God Reality. Well, guess what? That disgrace is coming to an end. Thank God!!! With the return of our Solar Christ Presence, the Twelve-fold Solar Flame of our Christ Presence is now blazing through our Heart Centers. It is activating our Twelve-fold Solar Spine and our Twelve-fold Solar Causal Body. The multi-dimensional, multi-colored frequencies of Solar Light are interpenetrating every atom and molecule of our four lower bodies, and as the Solar Light spins out from our Heart Flame, It fills the space between the electrons and sub-atomic particles of our bodies at an atomic cellular level.

This activity of Light is lifting us up in vibration into an octave of timelessness and spacelessness. This is giving our Solar God Presence the opportunity to reweave the Twelve Solar Strands of DNA, thus reconnecting our communication system with the Realms of Illumined Truth and Knowledge and our God Presence. This is happening gradually, according to the Divine Plan of each individual.

As we begin to reconnect the circuits of DNA, we begin to experience glimpses of "inner knowing." Before long we will be permanently reconnected with our Sun Being. Then, we will not have to depend on our limited lower human consciousness or anyone else's interpretations of truth. We will know that we know that we know, and our time of floundering in ignorance and darkness will be over.

We will know that all life is interrelated, and we will know that we cannot hurt any part of life without it reflecting back on us. We will know that the supply of the Universe is limitless, and we will know that the Earth is merely a reflection of Humanity's consciousness. We will know that poverty, hate, pain, suffering, disease, prejudice, evil, aging, death and all other forms of mutated energy are human miscreations that are not a necessary part of our Earthly experience. And we will know that Heaven on Earth is not only a viable option, it is a *very tangible, imminent reality.*

As the Twelve Solar Strands of DNA are rewoven within us and the Light filaments are reconnected through the Twelve Solar Helixes, the short circuit that disconnected us from the Realms of Illumined Truth and Knowledge will be spliced in a way that will automatically activate the pre-encoded memories of all the knowledge and truth we have ever known. The trick is that we, and the masses of Humanity, have to get our heads above the mud puddle of pain, suffering and fear long enough to raise the frequency of our bodies sufficiently for the reweaving of our Twelve Solar Strands to occur.

We are receiving welcomed assistance from on High to help us accomplish this tremendous feat. The Feminine Polarity of God, the essence of Divine Love, is pouring into the Planet as never before. It is awakening the right brain hemisphere and opening the Heart Center. This activity of Light is balancing our rational, logical mind (left brain) with our creative, intuitive mind (right brain), and it is balancing the Power Center of our Throat with the Love Center of our Heart. When this balance effectively occurs, our Power is always balanced with Love. This instills within us a perpetual Reverence for all Life, and it safeguards against our abuse of Power. When we are continually expressing our Power, embraced in the Divine Quality of Love, the distorted behavior patterns of aggression, dominance, greed, corruption, inhumanity, crime, violence, war, prejudice, hate, etc., will be non-existent.

We are going through a very special initiation at this time in which the Stargate of the Heart is being opened. This allows each of us to connect with the Heart of God, opening a permanent portal of Divine Love from the Realms of Perfection into the physical reality of Earth. The opening of the Stargate of the Heart allows Humanity's feeling nature to be lifted upward. This enables our feelings to be refocused, changing the power of our attention from fear to Abounding Joy. This shift of consciousness alone will make a tremendous difference in our frequency of vibration, and it will move us a quantum leap forward.

The critical need of this momentous hour is for the masses of Humanity to awaken to the opportunity at hand. This Blessed Planet and all Her life are Ascending from the third dimensional experience of a limited time-space continuum into the Fourth Dimensional experience of an unlimited timeless, spaceless, Solar Reality. This is the next evolutionary step of our Solar System. Unfortunately, the magnitude of just what this Ascension means is beyond the comprehension of our finite human minds. Consequently, we don't "get it," and we don't understand how to implement the concept of it into our everyday realities. It, therefore, just becomes a lofty platitude to the majority of people, and because it doesn't seem real, they don't benefit from the Abounding Joy of realizing Heaven on Earth is an imminent reality.

Ascension is a quality of the Fourth Solar Aspect of Deity. It is the radiance of this Solar Aspect that is bathing the Planet and flooding the consciousness of Humanity with the frequencies of the Ascension Flame. It has been determined by the Godhead that, due to the fact that most of Humanity is still immersed in the quagmire of pain and suffering, the frequencies of Ascension are vibrating above what our conscious mind can grasp. Consequently, this gift of Light is not having the positive effect that was expected. To remedy this problem, a contingency plan has been set into motion. It has been determined by the Company of Heaven that the influx of the Ascension Flame needs to be stepped down into a frequency that resonates clearly through the Heart of every man, woman and child on Earth, regardless of their level of consciousness or fear. The quality of the Fourth Solar Aspect of Deity that fits that particular qualification is known as HOPE.

Through a Divine Activity of Light projected through the

Cup of Humanity's consciousness, the entire Company of Heaven magnetized from the very Heart of our Father-Mother God the glorious *Wellspring of Eternal Hope.* This Holy Light was anchored into this Sweet Earth during the Sacred Conclave of Group Avatar, September 25-October 1, 1993, which was held in St. Augustine, Florida. This Divine Wellspring of Eternal Hope is now blazing through the open Stargate of the Heart of all Humanity, and It is secured within the Divine Momentum in the center of the Earth to continually bubble up through the waters and the crust of the Earth, bathing every electron of precious life energy evolving on this Planet.

This Wellspring of Eternal Hope is allowing the consciousness of Humanity to be lifted up once again, and It is enabling us to remember who we are. The masses are awakening to the fact that they are Sons and Daughters of God, and they are, once again, becoming receptive to the possibility of Transformation—Transformation of their own lives of pain, Transformation of the collective Family of Humanity and Transformation of Beloved Mother Earth.

The Wellspring of Eternal Hope is causing people to open their Hearts and Minds. It is stirring within them the need for truth and the need to connect with other Lightworkers on the Planet, so that they will feel Loved and supported in their newfound wisdom and hope.

It is imperative that each Lightworker be a Peace Commanding Presence of Love, a safe Haven whereby those awakening souls who are drawn to your sphere of influence may take a drink from your cup in an atmosphere of acceptance, tolerance, integrity, safety and above all, Divine Love. It is time that the truth be made readily available to all seekers. And, it is time that every seeker be given the space to determine his/her own truth through Divine Discerning Intelligence.

Ask the Presence of God blazing in your Heart to magnetize into your Forcefield of Light any seeker of truth who can benefit in any way from your Love and your truth. Then, in humble

Gratitude, give them a drink from your cup *with no expectations and absolutely no strings attached.*

As awakening souls experience the Wisdom and Knowledge of the Ages, they will be lifted higher and higher until their Twelve Solar Strands of DNA are rewoven, and the direct connection with their own multi-dimensional God Self and the Realms of Illumined Truth will be complete. Then, they will not have to depend on any outside source for their information or truth, and your service to them will have been accomplished God Victoriously.

Recently, I was given a graphic demonstration of the hunger for truth that is awakening within Humanity's Heart, and I came to a very clear realization. My friend, Kay Meyer, and I were invited to Toronto, Canada, to give a seminar. We never charge a fee, but we have always requested that our expenses be covered. These expenses add up to quite a bit since they include our air travel, hotel room, food, rental for meeting space, plus all of the expenses involved informing people of the seminar: mailing flyers, newspaper and radio announcements, posters, printing, brochures, handouts, long distance calls, etc. We always offer a *free*, open lecture the evening before our full-day seminar because I want to experience the joy of personally connecting with as many Lightworkers as I possibly can, even if they are unable to attend the seminar.

During the free, open lecture in Toronto, I experienced, for the first time, something that was intolerable for me. Many beautiful people who were obviously in pain, both emotionally and physically, came up to me after the lecture and expressed the deep regret that they could not afford to attend the seminar. These precious souls, with open Hearts, were desperately seeking some answers and a Ray of Hope that would ease their burden and enable them to continue their Earthly commitment to its God Victorious conclusion. The truth is here. The answers are available. But, they did not have access to them because of a monetary limitation.

I had nothing to do with the money end of it, and I did not have the authority to waive the registration fee because of the agreement I had made with our very Loving and committed sponsors. In that situation, I had no other option but to turn these precious people away. I did, however, in that very instant, vow to myself that *never again* will I be responsible for turning truth seekers away from the valuable information pouring forth from the Realms of Illumined Truth because they can't afford the price of admission.   Once I made that vow, the Stargate of my Heart burst open. An inner knowing surfaced into my conscious mind, and I knew that all was in Divine Order. I felt, deep within my Heart, that the limitless flow of God's Abundance would prevail. I made a Heartfelt commitment to offer my seminars FREE to anyone who feels drawn to attend.

I talked to Kay about it, and we agreed on a plan. We decided that we will offer four all-day seminars a year in various parts of the country. These seminars will coincide with the Solstices and the Equinoxes, so we will have one in December, March, June and September. We will ask our Beloved Friends and Lightworkers in the specific and surrounding areas to assist us in getting the word out. Hopefully, through this process, thousands of Lightworkers and truth seekers will come together to join Hearts and Minds in a unified effort to heal themselves and this Sweet Earth with all Her life.

The Wellspring of Eternal Hope will expand as the knowledge of Planetary Transformation and the Divine Intervention now occurring is brought to the conscious minds of the masses. As multitudes of Humanity learn and express the truth of a New Heaven and a New Earth, the Ascension of this Blessed Planet will be greatly accelerated. The necessary "critical mass" will be easily reached, and the consciousness of Reverence for ALL

Life will sweep Humanity into the embrace of Eternal Peace.

After this inner Heart commitment was made in Toronto, some friends invited Kay and me to visit the CN Tower. This is a beautiful tower in Toronto that is the tallest free-standing structure in the World. It is a communication tower, and as we stood aloft viewing the spectacular vista of Toronto, Beloved Mother Mary reflected in my Heart. *"As symbolically represented in this structure, it is time for the highest octaves of Truth to now be freely communicated to the World."*

Kay and I decided that instead of having people in various areas sponsor our seminars, The New Age Study of Humanity's Purpose would cover all of the expenses. We believe, beyond a shadow of a doubt, that God's Supply is limitless. And we know that the Light of God is *always* Victorious. Consequently, we accept God's flow of Abundance, and we absolutely know that all of the financial support we need to accomplish this Divine Plan will be made tangibly available into our hands and use.

All of the seminars will be held on a Sunday, and the seminars will be from 10:00 a.m. to 4:00 p.m. We will talk about all of the wonderful things that are taking place at inner and outer levels, and we will give practical, tangible tools that will enable us to transform our lives and manifest Limitless Physical Perfection. The first FREE seminar was held in Southern California on December 5, 1993.

If you would like to help us in any way, please let us know. We will gratefully accept any assistance you can give. We need people to help us distribute flyers, arrange public service announcements on radio and in the newspapers, spread the information to groups and organizations and, of course, financial assistance. We are a 501(c)3 non-profit organization, so your Love Offerings will be tax deductible. At this special time, any gift of ourself that we expend to spread the truth and the Light of God on Earth, whether it is time, energy or money, is greatly appreciated by the Heavenly Realms, and our gifts are lovingly expanded on their return to us. Our humble efforts are eternally inscribed in our Book of Life, and our rewards are infinite. We ask that the entire Company of Heaven expand ALL your gifts a thousand times a thousand-fold.

You may contact me through the following avenues:

Phone: (602) 885-7909
FAX: (602) 323-8252
Address: The New Age Study of Humanity's Purpose
          P.O. Box 41883
          Tucson, AZ 85717

I want to express my overwhelming gratitude to you for volunteering to be on Earth during Her sacred time of rebirth, and I want to thank you for all you are and all you do.

I Love you!!!

VISUALIZATION OF HOPE

A new Forcefield of Eternal Hope has been established on this Sweet Earth, and It is moving all life evolving on this Planet into an awakened state of consciousness. Within this new level of awareness, we will each realize our own Divinity. Once that truth registers in our minds and Hearts at a deep octave of KNOWING, never again will we flounder in the illusion of worthlessness and low self-esteem.

We have been getting brief flashes of our true God Reality for a period of time now, but this is different. This is a paradigm shift of consciousness that is taking place through every conceivable plane of intelligence. It is reaching into the depths of the mass hypnosis of Humanity that has held us repressed in the bondage of hopelessness, limitation and despair. It is permeating the smothering sea of human miscreation that surrounds the Earth and prevents us from breathing in the Holy Breath of God.

It is rending asunder the "veil of maya" that has blinded us from the Realms of Illumined Truth. It is calming the roar of Humanity's pain, so that we will once again hear the still, small voice of the God Presence within, as well as the music of the spheres and the silence of the Great Solar Quiet. And It is flowing in, through and around every electron of precious life energy that comprises the physical manifestations in the world of form, thus lifting every particle of life into a higher frequency of harmony, balance and Limitless Physical Perfection.

It is not necessary for us to fully understand all of the specifics of the Forcefield of Eternal Hope, but we are curious creatures, and we can usually focus more effectively if we have a visual description to image in our mind's eye while we are invoking the Light. Consequently, the Company of Heaven has revealed to us a facet of the magnificence of this Forcefield. A Tremendous Sapphire Blue triangle has been formed between Washington, D.C., St. Augustine, Florida and Tucson, Arizona by God's First Ray of Protection to create an invincible Forcefield of Protection around the Holy Brazier that cradles the Forcefield of Eternal Hope. Within the Sapphire Blue triangle pulsates a glorious Pink Sun of Divine Love. This Pink Sun represents the open Stargate of the Heart of Mother Earth and all Her life. Ever so gently, within the Pink Sun of Divine Love, formed out of the substance of Divine Love Itself, are beautiful Pink rose petals of truly gossamer Light. Within the center of this scintillating rose is a resplendent Swan that has been formed from the transcendent multi-dimensional frequencies of the Opal Ray of Transformation. The Swan has always symbolized transformation from the "ugly ducking" into the Swan of incomparable beauty. This special symbol now represents the transformation of Humanity, Mother Earth and all Her life into the wonder and awe of Heaven on Earth.

The Opalescent Swan of Transformation is actually the Brazier that holds the cascading Fountain of multi-colored Light in the physical plane of Earth. This fountain is the WELL-

SPRING OF ETERNAL HOPE, and It is truly a multi-dimensional activity of Light that extends from the highest Octaves of Perfection into the depths of Humanity's miscreations.*

This Gift of Eternal Hope is an aspect of the Ascension Flame that has the capability of reaching into even the most hardened Heart. There It will stir into remembrance the pre-encoded knowledge and wisdom from the Divine Mind of God that is pulsating in our Heart Flame. This knowledge and wisdom is then transmitted into our conscious mind and physical experiences through the Twelve Solar Strands of our DNA structures. It contains within It all that we need to know to fulfill our purpose and reason for being. It contains all of the skill, courage and confidence to act on that purpose. It contains the trust and integrity necessary to fulfill our purpose, according to the Divine Plan, with Reverence for all Life and the constant desire for the manifestation of the highest good for all concerned.

This Divine Knowledge and Wisdom contains within Its frequencies all we have ever known and the Divine impulse and blueprint of all we will ever be. By awakening this truth in every Heart Flame, it will be impossible for a single soul to believe that harming another part of life will somehow benefit his/her own selfish intent. It will be impossible for us to rationalize ourself into a lifestyle of poverty, crime, war, disease, loneliness, fear, stress, frustration, boredom, prejudice, hatred, failure and all of the other painful experiences we have created through our own ignorance.

The Forcefield of the WELLSPRING OF ETERNAL HOPE is a gift from God to help us during this unparalleled Cosmic Moment. This Gift of Eternal Hope will greatly accelerate our awakening, and It will lift us up out of the chaos and confusion long enough to grasp the opportunity at hand. Once we connect with the truth of transformation instead of the illusion of pain

*See depiction of this Forcefield on the cover of the book. Artwork by Sharon Maia Nichols.

and suffering, then pain and suffering will no longer have to be part of our Earthly experience. **It's that simple**. I know that sounds too easy, but truth is simple. We have only made life complicated because of our lack of understanding.

In order to benefit from the cascading Fountain of Eternal Hope that is now bathing the Planet, we don't have to fully believe or even understand everything about It. All we have to do is be willing to allow this gift from God to flow through us. Once It does, It will be part of our life experience, and we will reap the benefits in spite of ourself.

Visualize a miniature replica of the Forcefield of Eternal Hope blazing in your Heart. KNOW that with every breath you take, the Divine Light is bathing every facet of your Being and flooding your entire sphere of influence with Eternal Hope. Then, project this multi-colored Light into the World and flood the Planet and all Her life with the Essence of Hope. See Beloved Mother Earth donning Her resplendent garment of Light. And see Her Ascending into Her Divine Birthright as Freedom's Holy Star—Heaven on Earth.

SACRED HEALING WATER

The information pouring forth from the Realms of Illumined Truth confirms the fact that this powerful time is providing each of us with a unique opportunity to complete our painful, dys-functional past, so that we can move forward into a life of Limitless Physical Perfection. This is a time we have all been inwardly longing for, but outwardly fearing would never come. Even though all of the prophesies foretold of this coming time when Heaven would manifest on Earth, it just seemed too miraculous to be true. But, here we are, right in the midst of the

Transfiguration of this Sweet Earth and all of the Lifeforms evolving upon Her, and we are being given the unprecedented privilege of assisting in this glorious process. As this Holy time unfolds, the assistance pouring forth from on High is being revealed to us step by step, and if we will accept and reverently utilize the Sacred Knowledge and Gifts of Assistance being offered to us, more will be unveiled from our Father-Mother God.

One of the most important aspects of assistance being offered at this time is the opportunity to heal and balance our Emotional Body. In order to fully understand just how significant that is, we must realize that *80 percent* of our energy is released through our Emotional Body. That means that of all of the thoughts, words, actions and feelings we have ever released in any embodiment, in any octave or dimension of existence, 80 percent is qualified with our feeling nature. Most of that energy has been charged with fear, doubt, pain, suffering, grief, loneliness, anxiety, frustration, stress, abandonment, rejection, low self-esteem, feelings of unworthiness, failure consciousness, etc. Spasmodically we may have experienced a glimpse of joy and happiness, but I think it was generally the exception rather than the rule. Our Emotional Body is continually pulsating with all of the feelings we have ever *felt*. Consequently, when we try to lift ourself up out of the pain and confusion of our past by *thinking* positively, we are bombarded with doubt and fear and the taunting voice of our lower human ego that consistently mocks us with, "Who do you think you're kidding? There is no way you can change. You are a worthless failure." Does that sound familiar?

Well, now we are being given an opportunity to Transmute all of the frequencies of discord recorded in our Emotional Body. As you can well imagine, when 80 percent of all of the energy we have ever released is Transmuted back into its original perfection of Light and harmony, our ability to change our life into an expression of Love, prosperity, fulfillment, purpose and joy will take a quantum leap forward.

We have discussed two very important factors that are influencing the purging and cleansing of our Emotional Body. One is the higher Fifth Dimensional frequency of the Seventh Solar Aspect of Deity that is now being projected into the Planet Earth from the Heart of our Father-Mother God. This Divine Light is being qualified with a vibration of the Sacred Violet Flame beyond anything we have ever been able to withstand. This Sacred Fire, known in the Realms of Perfection as the Violet Flame of Limitless Transmutation, is designed to enter the core of every single electron of energy that has ever been misqualified by the evolutions of Earth. This sacred Fire awakens the Divine Blueprint, the Immaculate Concept recorded in that core, and It then pushes to the surface, for Transmutation, any frequency of vibration that conflicts with that Divine Blueprint. The Violet Flame of Limitless Transmutation purifies the negative vibrations as they surface and changes the frequency of the energy from discord back into harmony and balance.

The Violet Flame of Limitless Transmutation is building daily and hourly; this Divine Light is being intensified each moment the maximum that Cosmic Law will allow. It is blazing in, through and around every electron of energy associated with the Emotional Body of every man, woman and child, whether they are in or out of embodiment. It is also penetrating deep into the emotional strata of Beloved Mother Earth, cleansing Her Emotional Body and the substance associated with the Emotional Body, which is the Water Element. This activity will continue until Beloved Mother Earth and all life evolving upon Her are wholly Ascended and Free.

Our relationship with all the Earth is shifting. Even our relationship with nature and our environment is changing. The Elemental Kingdom is cooperating with us in this process of planetary healing, and we are being given a special gift by the Heavenly Realms at this time. This gift consists of the *physical activation* of the Water Element on Earth. This is the substance that comprises 98 percent of our Emotional Body and the Emotional Body of Mother Earth. This activation is an activity of Light that will immensely accelerate the Ascension of our four lower bodies into the Light Body of our Solar Christ Presence. This activation will also accelerate the Ascension of Beloved Mother Earth into Her Light Body. The acceleration of vibration of all physical, manifest form is the *key* to our Ascension into the octaves of Limitless Physical Perfection.

The Sacred Gift of this activation of Light through the Water Element is being projected initially through all of the Sacred Healing Springs on Earth. Throughout the history of time, water has been used as a Holy Sacrament, whether it has been for baptism, healing, cleansing or the "fountain of youth." Healing Waters have been discovered all over the World, and Humanity has continually flocked to the source to partake of the healing properties of the water. Often, because of distance, the Healing Waters were inaccessible to the masses, and consequently, most people were denied the privilege and honor of receiving the blessings of the Healing Water. Now, during this unprecedented time, the entire Company of Heaven is requesting that the activated Healing Waters of Earth be made readily available to *all* Humanity. In our humble way, we are committed to fulfilling that Divine Fiat. We have gathered Sacred Water from our Earthly journeys, and other Lightworkers have sent us Healing Water from Sacred Sites all over the World. In unision with the Company of Heaven, we have activated it and consecrated it to the fulfillment of the Divine Plan on Earth. The Realms of Illumined Truth have provided us with a specific activation process that will enable us each to consecrate and activate as much water as we desire by using a small amount of the Source Water from the Healing Springs. The water we activate through this process then becomes empowered with the full-gathered momentum of the original Healing Water, and we can use that water to empower and activate as much additional water as we like. This actually means that we can receive the benefits of the Healing Water for the rest of our life if we choose to continue the simple activation process. We can also have plenty of Healing Water to share with our friends and Loved ones. As we teach them the activation process they, too, can pass the gift of Healing Water on to their friends and Loved ones. The effect will be exponential, and very rapidly the healing blessings will cover the Earth, greatly enhancing and accelerating our Ascension into the Light.

We would like to make this Healing Water available to anyone who wants it. We offer it to you as a gift of Love and ask only that you revere this Sacred Elemental Substance, and do not buy or sell it. If you are inwardly directed to pass the Healing Water on to friends or Loved ones, please do so as a gift of Love.

If you would like to receive an Activated Starter of the Healing Water, please write to us, and we will send you a small bottle of the water. This water, which is a blend from the following Sacred Healing Springs, is to be activated into pure Spring Water or as close as you can come to that purity of water.

SOURCES OF THE HEALING WATER

MEXICO AND CENTRAL AMERICA

MEXICO: Tlacote, Palanque, Chichen Itza, Res Zapotes, Caribbean, Gulf of Mexico, Aqua Sol.
GUATEMALA: Tikal, Kaminal Juyu (at the same pyramid), a Sacred lake in the volcanoes, a Mayan Sacred Initiation Water-fall high in the mountains, St. Francis Cathedral.
HONDURAS: Copan.
COSTA RICA: Fountain of The Black Madonna.

EUROPE

ENGLAND: Chalice Well and Glastonbury Abbot, Stonehenge, Avesbury, Silbury Hill, Crop Circles, Blagdon Lake, St. Michael's Mont (English Channel).
SCOTLAND: Loch Ness, Callanish, Iona Abbey.
IRELAND: Blarney Stone, New Grange, Knowth, Downth, Hill of Tara, Hill of Slane; Holy Well of Mary, Kenmore, County Kerry.
FRANCE: Lourdes (The Miraculous Grotto), Rennes-le-Chateau St. Magdalene Church, Rennes-le-Bains, Mt. Bugurach, Carnac, Mont Saint Michel (English Channel).
PORTUGAL: Fatima.
ITALY: St. Peter's Basilica and St. Peter's Fountain at the Vatican, Basilica of St. Francis at Assisi, Mt. LaVerna.
SPAIN: Christopher Columbus Monument-Barcelona Harbor; Olympic Fountain at Olympic Village, Barcelona; Cathedral Santiago de Compostela, Finisterre at Galico, Spain.
BOSNIA-HERZEGOVINA: Medjugorje.

MIDDLE EAST

ISRAEL: Church of the Holy Sepulchre, Church of the Dormition on Mt. Zion, Garden of Gethsemane, Church of Mary Magdalene, Dome of the Rock, Western Wall (Wailing Wall), Sea of Galilee, Mt. Hermon, Mt. Beatitudes, Nazareth Church of Annunciation.

ASIA

GEORGIA: (Of the former Soviet Union).

AFRICA

EGYPT: Nile River, Initiation Wells at Karnak/Luxor, Dandara

and Abydos; Coptic Monastery of the Holy Virgin St. Mary; Church of Disciples, Monastery of St. Antony; St. Mark Coptic Church at Cairo and Alexandria.
REPUBLIC OF SOUTH AFRICA: Sacred Zulu Healing Water from the Indian Ocean.

NORTH AMERICA

USA: Manitou Springs - the Garden of the Gods, Colorado; Squaw Valley, Snake River, Idaho; Mt. Shasta, California; Hot Springs - Hot Springs National Park, Arkansas; Grand Tetons, Old Faithful, Yellowstone River, Wyoming; Oak Creek - Sedona, Montezuma's Well, Arizona; Mormon Temples at Salt Lake City, Utah and Independence, Missouri; El Santuarro De Chimayo, New Mexico (Lourdes of America); Basilica of the National Shrine of the Immaculate Conception in Washington, D.C.; Ponce de Leon's Dream Fountain of Youth, St. Augustine, Florida; Activated Water on the full moon Lunar Eclipse and Neptune/Uranus Conjunction, New Hampshire and North Carolina; Christ in the Hills, Kilgore, Ohio; Grotto of Our lady of Lourdes, Euclid, Ohio; Healing Water, Conyers, Georgia; Deer Park, Carlstadt, New Jersey (Holy Water activated on the new moon, January 11, 1994, during the unique Planetary alignment of the Planets Neptune, Uranus, Mercury, Venus, Mars, Sun and Moon, all aligned within a 9° span in the Sun Cycle of Capricorn).
CANADA: Mt. Robson, Lake Louise, Lake Lorraine—all associated with Archangel Michael.

SOUTH AMERICA

BOLIVIA: Three springs on the Island of the Sun at Lake Titicaca; St. Francis Church of Copacabana.
PERU: River of the Sacred Valley at Machu Pichu.
VENEZUELA: The Spring of Apparitions of the Virgin Mary,

Betania.

ECUADOR: Water Activated on the full moon Lunar Eclipse and Neptune/Uranus Conjunction.

This Sacred blend of Healing Water has been activated with the Divine endeavor of manifesting Limitless Physical Perfection on Earth, here and now. It has been charged with the concentrated Sacred Fires of Limitless Transmutation (Violet), Limitless Abundance (Gold), Limitless Healing (Green), Limitless Divine Love (Pink) and the full power of the Ascension Flame (White).

Limitless Physical Perfection means the literal Transfiguration of our physical realities into Heaven on Earth. This includes the restoration of our physical bodies into Vibrant Health, Eternal Youth and Radiant Beauty. It includes the transformation of our life experiences into expressions of Abundance, Loving Relationships, Fulfilling Jobs, Financial Freedom, Joy, Happiness, Eternal Peace, Reverence for ALL Life and all of the Glory of Heaven.

As you consume this Sacred Blend of Healing Water each day, do so as a Holy Sacrament, knowing and expecting that with every breath you take, your physical experience on Earth is being returned to God's original Divine Intent of Heaven on Earth.

All of the Healing Springs on Earth are being activated by the Realms of Perfection at this time to assist Humanity in our "hour of need." If you have access to a Healing Spring that is not included in our Sacred Blend of Water, please send us a small bottle of the water and a brief description of the information available about the Spring. We will check with our Heavenly Source to see if it is appropriate to add to our Activated Starter Water.

We need to truly grasp the magnitude of this opportunity. Every drop of activated water is empowered to activate *every* molecule of water it comes in contact with. This literally means that one drop of activated water has the power to activate an ocean into the full strength of the original Healing Spring. With this understanding, we realize that we can activate all of the rivers, lakes, streams, creeks, ponds, oceans and other bodies of water on the Planet. We can activate our swimming pools and spas, our bath water and our drinking water. The expansion of this gift of healing is limited only by the limits of our imagination.

When you order your Activated Starter Water you will be sent specific instructions on how to activate an ongoing supply of water for yourself and your Loved ones. Please copy the information and distribute it to everyone you share the Healing Water with, so they will know how to maintain their supply of Healing Water and how to teach others to activate their own water as well.

This is a time for each of us to go within our Heart, and ask for Divine Revelation and Guidance as to how this Sacred Gift can assist us in fulfilling our Divine Plan on Earth. Then, respond according to your inner Heart Call.

We have made a Heart commitment to make the Sacred Blend of Healing Water available to everyone who desires to receive it. It will be distributed free of charge to anyone who asks. Needless to say, there will be several expenses involved, such as bottles, packaging material, postage, printing, paper, etc. If you would like to assist us in sponsoring this Divine Directive from the Heavenly Realms, we will gratefully accept your Love Offerings. And, we invoke the Entire Company of Heaven to expand your financial gifts a thousand times a thousand-fold as that energy returns to you.

To order the Healing Water just write to:
The New Age Study of Humanity's Purpose, PO Box 41883, Tucson AZ 85717. Your Love Offerings may be sent to the same address. (We are registered as a 501(c)3 non-profit organization, so your contributions are tax deductible.)

THE ACTIVATED HEALING WATER
AND OUR EMOTIONAL BODY

An EXPANDED OPPORTUNITY is being presented through the Activated Healing Water to further heal the pain, grief, sadness, anger, fear, loneliness and failure consciousness stored in our feelings and Emotional Body. As you know, during the Summer Solstice of 1993, the Violet Flame of Limitless Transmutation, from the Fifth Dimensional Realms of Perfection, was anchored into the center of the Earth through the interdimensional "doorway" over the Caribbean Islands. This Sacred Fire, reflecting the Divine Love Nature of the Feminine Aspect of Deity, purged the dysfunctional emotional energies of mass consciousness from the body of Mother Earth. This facet of our Mother God sweeps away the old, so that the birth of the new can occur. This is a necessary part of Earth's Ascension, but because of our sometimes stubborn resistance to change, this purification often seems harsh. If we will recognize the unique opportunity at hand and willingly let go of our outmoded ways of thinking, feeling and acting, this inherent Power of Transmutation, the Divine Love of our Mother God, will be a welcome blessing. She is offering us a precious gift. She is preparing us for the next step of our evolution and Spiritual Initiation. She is preparing the way for our ultimate expression of Oneness and Totality. She is paving the way for our Ascension into the Heart of God.

We have all heard the horror stories of the predicted cataclysms that are supposed to take place during the purification of the Earth. Everything from devastating earthquakes to a holocaust nuclear war have been predicted. It is imperative for us to understand that the severity of this purification is *totally dependent* on our response. The TRUTH is that there are millions of awakened and awakening souls in embodiment this very moment who are on Earth for the explicit purpose of Transmuting the surfacing negativity by invoking Light into every discordant situation. This activity of Light is designed to calm the negativity and AVERT THE PREDICTED DISASTERS. As we utilize the Divine Love of the Violet Flame of Limitless Transmutation and project It into all negativity in the Earth, on the Earth or in the atmosphere of Earth, we will dissipate the destructive force of the negative energy and soften the outer world effects of the cleansing.

At the present time, the Emotional Strata of the Earth is being purified. This includes our Emotional Body, our feeling world and the Emotional Body of Mother Earth, all of which are reflected through the Water Element. When we resist letting go of the "old" consciousness of limitation to make room for the "new" consciousness of Divine Love and Enlightenment, we experience a backlash of that resistance, and the purification is intensified until we "see the Light" and release our outmoded ways of thinking, feeling and acting. The more willing we are to let go and move forward into the Light, the less cataclysmic the Earth changes will be.

Recently, we experienced some of the resistance of letting go, and as a result, we are witnessing the backlash of the Water Element on Earth. Again, the water reflects the Emotional Bodies of Humanity and Mother Earth. Since the purging over the Summer Solstice of June 21, 1993, we have seen unprecedented flooding in the Midwest U.S.A., Bangladesh, Nepal and India, as well as other parts of the world. It is interesting to note that in the U.S.A., this intense flooding occurred in the area that is most often called the "Bible Belt." I know there are many, many powerful, illumined souls in that area, but the "Bible Belt" is often perceived by the rest of the country as the area most resistant to change.

We have come to Love this Sweet Earth Free, and as the first impulse of cataclysmic purging appears on the Screen of Life, it is time for us to "walk our talk." The Light of God is ALWAYS Victorious, and we have the *absolute* ability to Transmute the negativity that is surfacing for purification BEFORE it manifests as a destructive force on the Planet. All we have to do is invoke the Light of God and accept the Sacred Gifts of assistance that are being given to us from on High.

One of the most empowered gifts of assistance is the activation of the Healing Waters around the World. This water has been distributed all over the World. Lightworkers have activated additional water and distributed it throughout their spheres of influence. The effect has been exponential, and now the Sacred Healing Water from the Healing Springs is blazing through oceans, lakes, rivers, waterways, drinking water, bathing water and the physical bodies of Humanity throughout the Planet.

This Sacred Healing Water has been greatly empowered and specially consecrated now by the Violet Flame of Limitless Transmutation. The Divine Love of our Father-Mother God has activated this blend of Healing Water to accelerate the healing of our Emotional Body and to accelerate the healing of the Emotional Body (Water) of Mother Earth. This Healing Water has the ability to dissipate the energies of cataclysms and disasters, and it will assist greatly in healing our body, mind, emotions and soul. Its power and effectiveness are being amplified daily and hourly by our Father-Mother God.

OUR HEALING WATER
IS A TANGIBLE SUCCESS

Our Sacred Blend of Healing Water is being used by thousands of Lightworkers around the Globe to heal the waters of the Earth. We were advised by the Beings of Light, in the Realms of Perfection, that now even greater assistance is being given from on High in order to accelerate the purification of the Emotional Body of Mother Earth (the Water Element) and the

Emotional Bodies of Humanity during this special time. This opportunity is initiating a New Order of Healing that is being permanently implemented on Earth.

Deep within our Heart we have always known that Beloved Mother Earth has the incredible capacity to heal Herself, if we will just invoke the Light and focus our attention on Her purification.

Some of our dear friends have been putting the Healing Water in the polluted Onondaga Lake in New York. They have been using the activation process that was given to us by the Spiritual Hierarchy. Recently we received the following letter with the enclosed newspaper article:

Dear Patti and Kay,

I am enclosing a newspaper clipping about Onondaga Lake. This lake is located here in the heart of the Syracuse, New York, area and has been declared the ***most polluted*** lake in the U.S., if not the world, by the scientific community. We have been taking the Sacred Healing water to the lake on a regular basis. Two weeks after we started this process the following article showed up in the newspaper.

What an affirmation of the power of the healing work. Lightworkers in the community are wearing permanent smiles and are dedicated to continue the work in this lake, as well as others in the area.

This lake is literally being resurrected from the dead.

Thank you, and God Bless you for sharing this information with all of us.

Love,
Carol

LIFE AT THE BOTTOM
Divers find light, green spots, 67 feet
below the surface of Onondaga Lake.

A diver scouring the deepest depths of Onondaga Lake startled scientists Friday with an unusual discovery: There's life on the bottom of the polluted lake.

For decades, scientists and other divers have described the bottom as a dark, lifeless abyss lined with toxic chemicals.

Now things seems to be changing.

Sandy Brown, a diver with a Canadian environmental company, reported seeing green spots, possibly algae, growing in toxic sediments about 67 feet below the surface.

"He said it looks like the bottom of Onondaga Lake has measles because there's all this green," said Jay Babin, a scientist from Waterloo, Ontario. He is one of four researchers working on a lake oxygen experiment.

Babin said the diver also was surprised to find sunlight reaching the bottom.

"When he went down, he said the water was fabulous. It was real clean down there. He said there was about 15-feet visibility," Babin said.

In the past, divers from local police and fire departments described the lower layers of the lake as dark and murky. Some divers said they couldn't see their hands in front of their faces.

Brown, dressed in insulated diving gear on Friday, didn't have a perfect trip. He found some evidence of Onondaga Lake's well-documented pollution problems.

Most notable was the layer of cloudy water about 10 feet above the bottom. In that layer, Brown tasted dangerous hydrogen sulfide, which rises from decaying matter in the sediments, Babin said.

Nevertheless, the diver found the very bottom of the lake was not as bad as it is reputed to be.

Several prominent scientists who study Onondaga Lake said they would like to take a closer look at the green spots and water.

Steven Effler, research director for the Upstate Freshwater Institute in Syracuse, is among those intrigued.

"Let's put it this way," Effler said while examing the dive site in a boat Friday. "We better find out what that stuff is. There isn't any oxygen down there."

(Newspaper article by Mark Weiner, Staff Writer.)

I don't believe it is an accident that this information is being brought to our attention. We are always being given encouragement from the Realms of Perfection to "keep on keeping on." Sometimes we become discouraged and feel overwhelmed by the enormity of the task at hand. What is being clearly revealed to us here is just how effective our humble efforts are and how powerful the tools are that are being given to us. After all, if the most polluted, dead lake in the World can begin coming back to life in just TWO WEEKS, imagine how quickly and Powerfully we are going to be able to heal other aspects of our life.

Keep Invoking the Light!
Keep using the tools!
Keep expressing Hope!
Keep expecting Healing!
Keep coming from Joy!
Keep Loving yourself!
Keep Loving Beloved Mother Earth
and ALL Her Life!
Remember, that is why you are here and your
VICTORY IS ASSURED!!!

THE DIVINE MOTHER PRINCIPLE,
THE FEELING NATURE OF GOD RETURNS TO
EARTH!

We are on the Dawn of Magnificence...
the Dawn of the Return of the feeling nature of God to
Earth...
the Dawn of the Divine Mother Principle

The Earth and all life evolving upon Her has experienced an unprecedented opportunity to heal the painful emotional energies of the past. Throughout 1993, the Earth was bathed in the celestial frequencies of Limitless Transmutation and Divine Harmony. This created a frequency of vibration that activated, within our atomic cellular structures, the pre-encoded patterns of our RNA-DNA blueprints. These patterns reflect the original Divine Intent of our feeling nature. We are now being given an opportunity to begin subtly perceiving new insights, which reflect the oneness of all life. Old beliefs of separatism and isolationism are being exposed as falsities and illusions. We have entered a glorious time in the evolution of Earth, which heralds a paradigm shift of consciousness into the REVERENCE FOR ALL LIFE.

This activity of Light enables us to lift up in consciousness, and we are now each being empowered with the multi-dimensional aspect of our Solar Christ Presence. This has occurred for every man, woman and child evolving on Earth, regardless of whether they were consciously aware of this gift or not. The Solar Christ Presence moves us beyond the limitations of our human ego, and It opens us up to the remembrance of our true human potential. The Solar Christ Presence infuses us with human dignity and independence, and It is heralding the birth of a new consciousness of Global Oneness. There is no turning back. Awakening within us is the knowledge and wisdom from the Divine Mind of God that enables us to remember clearly who we are and why we are here. We are Sons and Daughters of God, and we have come to Earth during the moment of Her rebirth to Love all life free. When I say "we" I am referring to every embodied human being.

1993 was a major turning point. Our direction and our purpose were renewed. We now have a greater sense of awareness and responsibility, and through the power of our focused attention, we are moving beyond all limiting circumstances. The Stargate of our Heart is opening; our right brain is being activated, and we are now physically prepared to receive the Celestial frequencies of the *feeling nature of God*. This Divine Plan was set into motion several years ago.

The feeling nature of God is projected through all creation on the Holy Breath of the Holy Spirit. The Holy Spirit is the Feminine Polarity of God expressed through Divine Love, and It is the aspect and Divine essence we now know as the Divine Mother Principle of our Father-Mother God. In order for us to experience the Divine feeling nature of God, which is always pulsating with perfect harmony and balance, it is critical that two factors be in place. The Stargate of our Heart must be opened, and our right brain hemisphere must be activated. With the integration of our Solar Christ Presence that took place in 1993, both of these things occurred, and we are now physically prepared to receive the harmony and balance of the feeling nature of God, the Divine Mother Principle.

On June 11, 1988, an activity of Light took place that began the initial impulse for this Cosmic Moment. Through a six hour event called Star∗Link 88, several thousand people gathered at the Los Angeles Coliseum in Los Angeles, California—the City of Angels. In unified consciousness, the Lightworkers physically present and those tuning in in consciousness from all over the world created a forcefield of Light that enabled a multi-dimensional doorway to be opened. This open portal allowed the Light of God to pour into Earth, and through this influx of Light, a reactivation and initiation into multi-dimensional awareness occurred in every human Heart. This blessed Planet and all Her life was lifted up yet another octave in vibration, closer to the Heart of our Father-Mother God.

Through the activity of Star*Link 88, the Angelic Host, from frequencies beyond anything we have ever experienced before, entered the atmosphere of Earth. These Mighty Solar Angels from the Fifth Dimension assisted God in activating the pre-encoded memories that were implanted deep within Humanity's cellular patterns aeons ago. These patterns reflect our Divine Plan, our purpose and reason for being.

A Cosmic Fiat was issued by the Godhead, and 1988 was decreed the year in which Humanity would step through the doorway into a multi-dimensional awareness. This was accomplished as the frequencies of the third dimension were accelerated closer to the higher octaves of the Fourth Dimension.

During that sacred moment in time, Humanity was empowered with the increased Presence of the Angelic Host from the Fifth Dimension Who are, even now, continually entering the Earth through the open Angelic Vortex in Los Angeles. The influx of Angels has formed an expanded bridge between Heaven and Earth—spirit and matter.

Angels are the messengers of God Who are specifically entrusted with the service of carrying the feeling nature of God, the Divine Love of the Holy Spirit, into the tangible world of form. The Light from these Ministering Solar Angels has been increasing daily and hourly. Moment to moment, the activated pre-encoded memories of our purpose and reason for being have been reverberating through our creative centers of thought and feeling.

This activity has been building in momentum for several years now. With the victorious return of our Solar Christ Presence and the purging of our Emotional Body and the emotional stratum of Earth which was accomplished in 1993, through the Neptune-Uranus Conjunction, all was in readiness for the next step of the Divine Plan. That step was re-establishing the feeling nature of God, the Divine Love of the Divine Mother Principle, permanently on Earth.

The return of the Divine feeling nature of God literally means that, at long last, we are being held in the nurturing, Loving Heart of our Mother God, as well as being embraced in the Divine Will and Power of our Father God. This balance is an *imperative* factor in our transformation. The loss of this balance was caused by the "fall of man," and we have been struggling and floundering in pain and ignorance for aeons of time as a result of being separated from the Divine Love of our Mother God.

I would like to briefly explain these two polarities of God so that we will all understand, with greater clarity, the significance of what the return of the feeling nature of God really means.

We often hear about the duality of God, the two opposite polarities, but we have seriously misunderstood this concept. Continually, the duality of God is being misinterpreted as *good and evil* or Light and darkness. People believe that these opposites are necessary in order to learn our lessons on Earth. They believe that we can't experience Love without hate, peace without war, prosperity without poverty, happiness without sadness, truth without deception, comfort without pain, health without disease, etc. Since we *know* that whatever we put our attention on, we bring into form, it becomes crystal clear that this particular belief system is perpetuating the negativity on Earth. As long as we believe that we can't experience the "good" without the "bad," then we will keep on creating the "bad."

The truth is that the "bad" was *never* intended to be part of our Earthly experience. That is why we were given the commandment by God to not partake of the Tree of Knowledge of Good and Evil. God gave us the gift of free will, and He/She knew that if we focused on evil (disease, hate, war, poverty, pain, etc.) with our creative faculties of thought and feeling, then we would bring evil into form and create these distorted experiences as part of our Earthly lessons. That was not the original plan.

The original plan was that we were to use our free will to learn to be co-Creators with our Father-Mother God and manifest Heaven on Earth, thus fulfilling the Universal Law of "As above, so below." Through our free will, we were to observe the multitude of Heavenly manifestations and choose which of the glorious expressions of God we would like to create on Earth. Then, by energizing that particular aspect of Heaven with our thoughts and feelings, we would project it onto the atomic structure of matter and bring it into physical form. In other words, our free will was not intended to be used to create the opposite experiences of good and evil, but rather, we were to use our free will to choose what aspect of Divinity we wanted to co-create with our Father-Mother God on Earth.

At a certain point in our evolution, we began experimenting with our gift of free will and began using it in ways that were not originally intended. We began creating thoughtforms and feelings that manifested as patterns other than the perfection of Heaven. As these distorted thoughtforms began to reflect on the physical substance of matter, fragmented patterns began to form that eventually mutated into what we now call the opposite polarity of perfection or "good." They mutated into the per-verted frequencies of "evil." Since we were responsible for these gross miscreations, a contingency plan was set into motion by God to give us the opportuntiy to learn just how painful the negativity of war, disease, poverty, hate, pain, etc., was, so that we would be motivated to Transmute the negativity back into its original frequency of peace, health, prosperity, love, comfort, etc. We have been learning our lessons through experiencing the pain of our miscreations for so long that we now believe that is what God intended for us to do in the first place. But, it is *not,* and it is only by accepting this fact and choosing to create Heaven on Earth exclusively that this unfortunate detour from our original path will be corrected.

Now, how did this diversion from the original plan affect the Divine Mother Principle? Well, in the beginning, the true

DUALITY of God, the Masculine Polarity and the Feminine Polarity of God were in perfect balance. The Masculine Polarity of God entered the left brain hemisphere as a blue shaft of Light and activated the Power Center of the Throat, projecting God's Will into the physical plane as It spiraled through the spinal column, activating the Masculine Polarity of the chakra system. The Feminine Polarity of God entered the right brain hemisphere as a pink shaft of Light and activated the Love Center of the Heart, projecting the feeling nature of God into the physical plane as It spiraled through the spinal column, activating the Feminine Polarity of the chakra system. When the two hemispheres of the brain are in perfect balance—the rational, logical left brain and the creative, intuitive right brain—then the Power Center of the Throat and the Love Center of the Heart are also in perfect balance. This means that our Power is always embraced with Love. When this is the case, it is impossible for us to inflict abuse on any other part of life because, in this balance, we experience a deep knowing of oneness and reverence for all life. We understand the unity of life and the interrelatedness of life. In this state of awareness, dominance, aggressiveness, violence, crime, abuse, deception, corruption and all other misuse of power becomes blatantly ignorant. Held in the *balance* of our Father-Mother God we know that we can't hurt any part of life without that reflecting back to hurt us in some way. Consequently, the abuse of power that we have experienced in every facet of life for millenia has been a ludicrous act of self-destruction.

When we began experimenting with our thoughts and feelings to create thoughtforms that were not reflecting the perfection of the Heavenly Realms, the pain we experienced as a result of this abuse of power was excruciating. To protect ourself from hurting so much, we began closing down our feelings and numbing ourself. *This caused the Stargate of our Heart to close down, and it also caused our right brain hemisphere to become almost dormant.* When this happened, the feeling nature of God, *the Divine Mother Principle, was withdrawn.* That left our Power Center unprotected. The negative effect of this tragedy was the unbridled abuse of power. To this very day, we can observe every single negative thing that is taking place on Earth and trace its origin back to the abuse of power and the lack of reverence for all life. With this insight, it becomes blatantly obvious that it is imperative for us to integrate the feeling nature of God once again into our Earthly experience. It is the ONLY way the rampant abuse of power can be quelled. It is ONLY through the Love of the Divine Mother Principle that reason and sanity can be brought back to shatter the mass hypnosis that has entrapped the consciousness of Humanity in fear and limitation. And, it is ONLY through balancing the Love of the Divine Mother Principle with our Power that we will accomplish our Divine Destiny, which is our Eternal Ascension into the Light.

As you can see, the return of the feeling nature of God is *monumental.* The magnitude of this event is truly beyond our comprehension. But, if we will go within to the deepest recesses of our Heart, we will begin to glimpse the overwhelming gratitude pouring forth from Heaven, and we will each feel the Loving embrace of our Mother God as Her words reverberate through our consciousness, "Well done, my beloved child. Your victorious accomplishment has assured My Eternal Presence on Earth. 'I Am' now and will always be with you."

The return of the feeling nature of God was accomplished through the unified efforts of every Lightworker on Earth over aeons of time, but the final permanent anchorage took place through a building momentum of Light that began on December 5, 1993, and culminated on the Winter Solstice on December 21, 1993. I was directed within my Heart to begin offering free seminars to share the Divine Knowledge pouring forth from the Realms of Illumined Truth with anyone who desired to receive It. I knew in my Heart that the first free seminar was to be held in Los Angeles within the Angelic Vortex and that it would be associated with the Winter Solstice of 1993. The seminar was scheduled for Sunday, December 5, 1993, 10:00 a.m. to 4:00 p.m. at the Bonaventure Hotel in downtown Los Angeles. As I prepared for the seminar, I felt, at times, overwhelmed with a sense of expectancy, and I knew that somehow this event was going to be the most profound activity I had experienced to date in my service to the Light. I knew it was associated with the Divine Mother Principle, and I knew that Humanity was in a state of readiness for the next paradigm shift due to the purging of our Emotional Bodies that had been taking place throughout the year. The specifics of the event had not been revealed to me yet, but through my experience, I knew I was to just rest in the embrace of trust. (I often say that I believe our Divine Plans are being fulfilled in spite of us, not because of us.)

For an eleven day period in November, 11-11-1993 (22) to 11-22-1993 (22), the Earth was bathed with an accelerated activity of the Violet Flame of Limitless Transmutation and Liberation. This Divine Essence flowed into Earth from the very Core of all Creation. The Goddess of Liberty, the Divine Being Who embraced the Earth in Her luminous Presence for the entire year of 1993, directed this Sacred Fire in, through and around every electron of energy on Earth, cleansing and liberating every particle of life from the remaining residue of painful emotional experiences of the past. This activity was the final push to heal our Emotional Bodies and the emotional strata of Earth the maximum that Cosmic Law would allow in preparation for the next phase of the Divine Plan.

On November 28, 1993, we experienced a total full moon Lunar Eclipse. This particular Eclipse was in full view in the Southwestern United States of America. It had several special features associated with it, and it was conjunct with the South Node. This combination of effects specifically dealt with the karmic debris that kept Humanity bound to the past. This unusual Eclipse set the stage for the unparalleled purification of the Etheric patterns of all of the negativity we have ever experienced as a result of the Divine Mother Principle withdrawing from the Earth plane aeons ago. This negativity consisted of all the abuse and neglect that has been inflicted on the feminine aspect of life in any way, shape or form since the "fall of man." It consisted of all the struggles women have endured as mothers and wives. It consisted of all oppression women have experienced in the way of degradation, humiliation, sexual abuse, lack of respect, lack of reverence, lack of honor and lack of Love. It also consisted of the invalidation and negation of women and their feminine qualities of intuition, creativity, nurturing and Love.

These discordant patterns, pulsating in the Emotional Bodies of Humanity and the emotional strata of Earth, have created the greatest and most effective block in preventing the return to Earth of the feeling nature of God, the Divine Mother Principle. The Lunar Eclipse, conjunct with the South Node, enabled these destructive patterns to be cut free from the atomic cellular substance of physical matter, and it allowed the liberation of these fallen patterns from the RNA/DNA blueprints of the third dimension. This prepared the fallen feminine energies to be victoriously Ascended back into the Light.

On December 2, 1993, my beloved mother made her transition into the Light through the process we call death. From outer appearances this seemed unexpected, but at inner levels, it was all part of the plan. As I began to release the initial shock and grief, I started to tap the truth of what was happening, and the Divine Plan began unfolding before me, step by step. Numerologically, 12-2-1993 works out to a 9 vibration, and my mother was 81 years old, which is also a 9 vibration. Nine is the number of completion, and it sets the stage for the cycle of rebirth and a new beginning.

In her outer human consciousness, my mother was not aware of the fact that she was a powerful force of Light on Earth. This is true of most Lightworkers at the present time, but fortunately, our God Presence is still effectively working through us. My mother was a sweet, humble lady who Loved her family and sacrificed herself beyond what was necessary. Often, when she and I were talking about normal everyday things, there would be such a powerful force of Light pouring through her into me that I could barely see her physical form on the other side of the room. I never shared that information with her because it seemed too sacred to talk about.

What was revealed to me after her transition was that she had volunteered to reach into the depths of the frequencies of what women have suffered since the closing of the Stargate of the Heart and the withdrawal of the feeling nature of God from Earth. She connected with these fallen feminine energies through her own difficult experiences as a woman, a wife and a mother. Her Earthly sojourn this time was very, very difficult, and it reflected the gamut of feminine struggles. Her children (two girls and two boys) watched her courage and her strength blended in the dichotomy of her co-dependency and what was sometimes perceived as weakness. Through it all, she never complained or felt sorry for herself.

As she walked through the pain of her life, she connected in energy, vibration and consciousness with the frequencies of every other woman, wife and mother who had experienced similar pain and abuse. The dysfunctional frequencies of fallen feminine energy were woven into her etheric patterns so that when she left the Earth plane, she would be able to draw those fallen energies up with her into the Octaves of Perfection. The law is, "As 'I Am' lifted up, all life is lifted up with me." As my mother proceeded through her transition into the Light, she created an upward rush of energy that allowed the liberated fallen feminine energy to be pulled up from the physical plane into the higher dimensions for purification. This process took three days. From December 2nd through December 4th, the Goddess of Liberty and the Legions of the Ascension Flame assisted in this activity of Light. As my mother pierced deep into the depths of feminine suffering, the Goddess of Liberty blazed the Flame of Liberation through all of the discordant patterns of female energy on Earth that were in any way blocking the return of the Divine Mother Principle. This sacred Flame Transmuted these patterns of abuse—cause, core, effect, record and memory. The liberated patterns were cut free from every person on the Planet, regardless of whether or not they were in a male or female body this time around. Then the Legions of the Ascension Flame poured forth the sacred substance of the Ascension. As my mother Ascended into the Octaves of Light, all of the liberated female energies were lifted back into their original Divine Intent. After this process was victoriously accomplished, all was in readiness for the return to Earth of the feeling nature of God, the Divine Mother Principle.*

On December 5, 1993, several hundred people gathered in Los Angeles, California within the forcefield of the Angelic Vortex. Lightworkers from all over the world joined with us in consciousness, and the Solar Christ Presence of all Humanity participated at inner levels. Throughout the six-hour seminar, Light from the very Heart of God poured through the Angelic Vortex into the cup of our unified consciousness. The Light was then projected into the crystal grid system of Earth. This Light of Divine Love from our Mother God created reinforcing grids of Love through all of the land faults in California and through all of the tectonic plates, faults and fissures in the body of Mother Earth, embracing this blessed Planet in an invincible forcefield of protection and Divine Love

This Light of Divine Love was projected into the right brain hemisphere of each person evolving on Earth. Then, It poured through the open Stargate of every human Heart into the physical plane. This created an expanded grid of Love permanently reconnecting every man, woman and child in the embrace of our Mother God. All was then in readiness for the return of

---

* *Rarely do I ever relate such a personal reference, but in my Heart, I feel that this information will help each of us to see the magnitude of what we, as Lightworkers, are capable of doing. We each have a very important mission, and our Light is limitless.*

the Archetype for the Divine Mother Principle.

The resplendent Presence of the Divine Mother Archetype was projected into the atmosphere of Earth from the very Heart of God through the open Angelic Vortex and through the open Stargate of every Heart. The Immaculate Concept of this Divine Blueprint was re-encoded in the genetic patterns of all life evolving on Earth, thus preparing each particle of life for the perfect balancing of the right and left brain hemispheres and the balancing of the Throat Center of Power and the Heart Center of Love.

This Blueprint of the Divine Mother Archetype built in power and momentum until the Winter Solstice, December 21, 1993. During that Cosmic Moment, the Archetype of the Divine Mother Principle was anchored through every Heart Flame into the center of the Earth for all Eternity, bringing to perfect God Victorious fruition the RETURN OF THE FEELING NATURE OF GOD, THE DIVINE MOTHER PRINCIPLE, TO EARTH!!!!

With the victory of this facet of the plan accomplished, we were truly ready for a glorious rebirth and Ascension into the next phase of the Divine Plan.

Capricorn begins on the Winter Solstice, which is the longest night of the year, and it is considered the most mysterious of all of the Sun Cycles. The Winter Solstice has always been perceived as the holiest night of the year, since it heralds the return of the Sun, the Light, to Earth. Light is the Law of Life. Capricorn represents the Essence of the Law. For millennia now Capricorn has reflected only the Patriarchal Law of the Father. This was the result of the tragic withdrawal of the Matriarchal energies of the Divine Mother Principle. As the imbalance of masculine energies began to overwhelm the Earth, the Patriarchal Law of the Father was misunderstood and misused by Humanity to dominate, manipulate and control life. In order for this Earth to regain Her rightful place in the Universe, this travesty must be corrected. This, in fact, was the next phase of the Divine Plan.

The first new moon following the Winter Solstice is considered extremely powerful because it symbolizes the Feminine Nature of God (represented by the Moon) assisting the Masculine Nature of God (represented by the Sun) to bring the Light (Sun) back to Earth. The first new moon following the Winter Solstice of 1993 was on January 11, 1994. January 11, 1994, was the second anniversary of a Cosmic Event called "Ascending through the Doorway of 11:11." For clarity, I will briefly describe that activity of Light.

The Doorway of Eleven:Eleven (11:11) was a term that referred to a span of time from July 11, 1991, to January 11, 1992. On July 11, 1991, the Earth went through a Cosmic experiment. This was an experiment that had never before been tried in any system of worlds, an experiment of unprecedented Divine Intervention. Every illumined soul in embodiment on Earth was prepared at inner levels while they slept at night to assist in the plan. We were each given an opportunity to renew our vows to Love all life on Earth free, which we had taken within the Heart of God before this embodiment. A new level of purpose and commitment began to filter into our conscious minds, and we began to intuitively perceive the urgency of the hour.

To assist in the experiment, Legions of Cosmic and Ascended Beings from the entire Universe descended into the atmosphere of Earth and took Their strategic positions around the Planet to embrace this sweet Earth in an invincible forcefield of Love and protection.

The experiment took place during a rare celestial alignment of the Sun, the Moon and the Earth, a unique Solar Eclipse that was held in the momentum of the new moon. Solar Eclipses occur fairly regularly on the Planet, approximately two per year, but the eclipse that took place on July 11, 1991, was rare in that it was a full seven minutes of total alignment. This unusual Solar Eclipse was held in the embrace of two full moon Lunar

Eclipses, one on June 26, 1991, and one on July 26, 1991.

During the seven minutes of the Solar Eclipse, in which the Sun, Moon and Earth were perfectly aligned, all of the pressures of imbalance, discord and karma were temporarily lifted from every cell, atom, electron and sub-atomic particle on the physical realm of Earth. During that Cosmic Moment, the only forces in action on the physical plane were the Fire Pillars of Love and Power of our Father-Mother God, blending in perfect balance, realigning the foundations of consciousness on Earth with Divinity. The central core of perfection that continues to beat within the Heart of every electron of life existing on Earth was activated.

The Solar Impulse of our Father-Mother God arced out of the Great Central Sun entering the physical Plane of Earth completely unopposed and unimpeded. The power of this sacred Light accelerated the core of perfection within EVERY atom. This profoundly affected the substance of organic/cellular life on Earth, particularly in the DNA and RNA in which the blueprint for the Planet's Divine Plan is recorded. This substance contains the plan of absolute perfection of the physical realm.

During the moment of the Solar Eclipse, our God Parents released a Violet Ray of Freedom that was the perfect balance of the Masculine Polarity of Divine Power—Sapphire Blue and the Feminine Polarity of Divine Love—Pink. The Violet Ray of Freedom, which was able to enter the Earth for the very first time unimpeded by negativity, TRANSMUTED INTO FOURTH DIMENSIONAL FREQUENCIES OF PERFECTION, 50 PERCENT OF ALL OF THE ENERGY THAT HAS EVER BEEN MISQUALIFIED ON EARTH. This energy was Transmuted mostly from unconscious and subconscious realms. This literally means that 50 percent of every electron of precious life energy we have ever misqualified in any existence or dimension, both known and unknown, through the misuse of our creative faculties of thought and feeling, IS GONE!!!

This negative energy has interpenetrated our Beings at a cellular level for aeons of time holding sway over our atomic vehicles. This is why disease and distress seem so prevalent in our human experience. With this purification, a re-alignment and re-balancing occurred at a deep atomic level. Now the Solar Healing of our God Parents will profoundly affect the living cells of Humanity and the Nature Kingdom, as well as the molecules, atoms, electrons and sub-atomic particles of all life within Earth's realms (animate and inanimate). This will accelerate the physics, chemistry and biology of life on Earth into Fourth Dimensional consciousness. In simple words, this Transmutation of negativity scientifically assures the Ascension of this Planet HERE and NOW! The effects of this cause will now allow each of us to more quickly rediscover our own Divine Plan, free from ONE-HALF of the old baggage from our past.

THE SOLAR INBREATH

With 50 percent of the mass karma of Humanity and the other lifewaves on Earth Transmuted, a door of opportunity opened during the eclipse to allow even greater assistance from on High. The purification of 50 percent of our past ensured the inclusion of the physical realm of Earth in a Solar Inbreath that involved our entire Solar System. A Solar Inbreath is a multi-dimensional activity of Light in which our Father-Mother God breathe all life closer to Their own Divine Three-fold Flame. This activity aligns all of the Three-fold Flames that pulsate in any form of life. The Three-fold Flame at any point of evolution is the focal point of unity with the whole of creation. Even though all forms of life evolve in different directions with different goals and different experiences, at certain points in each great Cosmic Cycle, all activity is suspended "for a Cosmic moment" to reconfirm that all life is ONE...and that this fundamental condition of the Universe remains primary and absolute!

This is termed a Solar Inbreath.

The Solar Inbreath connotes a movement in toward the center. When we breathe, we breathe in toward our Heart Flame, and so do our God Parents. But this Solar Inbreath occurred not in the physical realm as measured by distance or time, rather, It occurred in the Realms of Consciousness where an alignment of all Three-fold Flames brought an accelerated magnetic cohesion amongst all the component parts. This reconfirmed that God's First Cause of Perfection for all life has complete dominion throughout the whole of creation. This is symbolized in physical terms as if the Planets are drawn closer to the Sun. What does occur for all Planets is a more perfect orbital pattern and accelerated core planetary vibration through the planetary Three-fold Flame. In the Earth's case, it also included a gentle, but sure, straightening of the planetary axis.

During the Solar Inbreath, the alignment of all Three-fold Flames was not just vertical (between the various realms and dimensions of this Universe) but also horizontal (within each realm and dimension). This is particularly true for the physical realm of Humanity. A certain fundamental alignment of all Three-fold Flames within Humanity was produced so "the whole of Humanity," through Her center, can rise into the Fourth Sphere of Unconditional Divine Love. This opportunity ended all separateness permanently...not only of Earth and Humanity from the Divinity of the Universe, but it also ended the separation of Humanity from the influence of our own Three-fold Flame of Cosmic Balance and Healing. Remember, the Three-fold Flame at the center of every human being is the same Flame in the Central Sun.

At the moment of the Solar Eclipse in 1991, and sustained thereafter, the Three-fold Flame of every human being (in and out of embodiment) was fundamentally changed, completely aligned with and further empowered by the Three-fold Flame of Alpha and Omega from the Great Central Sun. This will allow each Three-fold Flame to now function like the Sun Itself and begin an Inbreath of all the energies of the four lower vehicles of each individual into the Sun or Christ Self...gradually, but very assuredly, raising all the energy and vibration of that lifestream into Fourth Dimension Consciousness.

The Three-fold Flame was to be the Source of all guidance and development of the Universe, including our own sphere of influence on Earth. In the history of Humanity's evolution, the source of guidance and authority shifted to the lower human ego, bringing about the present difficult and painful experiences now related to physical embodiment. However, there shall now be a fundamental shift back to the Three-fold Flame as the Source of all guidance and authority for Humanity's development. The Solar Eclipse/Inbreath in 1991 was God's mark of this shift.

The effects of the Solar Eclipse built in momentum until January 11, 1992. We were told by the Realms of Truth during Harmonic Convergence that the move into the Fourth Dimension would be a 25-year process beginning on August 17, 1987. The first five years would be the most tumultuous as the purging was accelerated. We would then go through a series of quantum shifts in vibration that would move us through the "doorway" from the third dimension into the Fourth Dimension, and it would take 20 years, until the year 2012, to complete the Ascension onto our new spiral of evolution. On January 11, 1992, the Earth and all Her life took a quantum leap into the frequencies of the Fourth Dimension and began the 20-year sojourn onto the next spiral of evolution. We victoriously passed through the "Doorway of 11:11."

The Realms of Truth revealed that there would be additional quantum shifts in vibration that would occur on each anniversary of January 11th until the year 2012, thus enabling us to Ascend further into the Octaves of Perfection step by step. We were told that each shift in vibration would be determined by how much Light had been effectively anchored into the Earth during the year and how successfully the Divine Plan for the year had been fulfilled.

January 11, 1994, was unequaled. Not only was it the first new moon following the unparalleled return of the Divine Mother Principle, which occurred on the Winter Solstice, but it also was empowered with a very, very rare alignment of Planets. On that sacred day, seven Planets (Mercury, Venus, Mars, Uranus, Neptune, the Sun and the Moon) were aligned within a nine-degree span in the Sun Cycle of Capricorn. That rare alignment was the most concentrated alignment of Planets in the last 300 years.

This alignment in the Sun Cycle of Capricorn during the Cosmic Moment of the return of our Mother God heralded the reinstatement of the BALANCE OF THE MATRIARCHAL LAW OF THE MOTHER on Earth.

On January 11, 1994, once again this sweet Earth and all Her life Ascended yet another quantum leap closer to the Heart of Perfection. This time the Earth was embraced in the perfect BALANCE OF THE LAW OF LIGHT OF OUR FATHER-MOTHER GOD. Held within this balance of Light, we were able to Ascend in consciousness into the Solar Heart of our Beloved God Parents in the Great, Great Central Sun, and here our Solar Christ Presence was invested with a Twelve-fold Solar Heart Flame. This literally means that the Three-fold Flame we have always experienced as our Divine Spark has now been empowered and expanded to reflect into all of our experiences the Twelve Solar Aspects of our Father-Mother God in PER-FECT BALANCE. *Our Heart Flame is now a Twelve-fold spiraling reflection of the Twelve Solar Aspects of Deity.* The Stargate of our Heart is now open to all Dimensions of Divinity, and as we evolve into this new level of Godhood, even the body of God is evolving, and our White Fire Being is now pulsating with the Twelve-fold Flame and the Infinite Causal Body of the Sun beyond the Sun beyond the Sun.

As we focus our attention on this truth, our God Presence will reveal to us the immensity of just how this will enhance our Earthly sojourn.

Our Ascension into the Light is steady and secure. There is no turning back, and our Victory is Assured.

What a sacred honor and privilege it is to be part of
this glorious plan.
We are ALL immeasurably blessed!

ASCENSION INTO THE
SOLAR CHRIST PRESENCE

We have "walked through the winter of our discontent" into the glory of a New Day filled with the full-gathered potential of Heaven on Earth.

Victory is Ours! Victory is Ours! Victory is Ours!

The Perfect Balance of Our Father-Mother God
and The Solar Christ Presence of Humanity
have RETURNED to Earth!!!

Hallelujah! Hallelujah! Hallelujah!

We each have the awesome responsibility of BECOMING the full manifestation of our Solar Christ Presence while we are still in embodiment on Earth. This literally means integrating the radiant luminous Solar Presence of our Holy Christ Self into our four lower bodies at an atomic cellular level, thus filling every electron, every atom, every sub-atomic particle of our bodies and all the space in between the atoms and molecules of our bodies with the multi-colored, multi-dimensional Light of our Solar Christ Presence. This will allow the higher aspect of our own Divinity to reclaim control of our physical, etheric, mental and emotional bodies. Once this occurs, our thoughts, words, actions and feelings will reflect only the Divine Love, Harmony and Balance of God. This transformation will have the effect of changing our physical realities into the Limitless Physical Perfection of Heaven on Earth. I know this seems too good to be true, but it is the Divine Fiat—the Cosmic Decree of our Father-Mother God that is now ringing through the Universe. It is a unique gift, a sacred opportunity being presented to every man, woman and child right here and right now.

VISUALIZATION FOR INTEGRATING THE SOLAR CHRIST PRESENCE

My eyes gently close, and "I Am" breathing easily and rhythmically. I feel the Divinity of my Heart expanding. (Pause...) My Solar Christ Presence Lovingly commands my lower human ego to release my four lower bodies:

"Human ego, I Love you, and 'I Am' grateful for the opportunity you have provided for me to grow and learn in this physical plane, but now I command you into the Light...

Human Ego...
Release my physical body NOW, and stand aside for the Christ.

Human Ego...
Release my etheric body NOW, and stand aside for the Christ.

Human Ego...
Release my mental body NOW, and stand aside for the Christ.

Human Ego...
Release my emotional body NOW, and stand aside for the Christ.

Human ego, I now command you into the Light, and I Love you Free into the higher schools of learning where you will be Transmuted into God's Perfection."

My Solar Christ Presence now steps into the full authority of my four Earthly bodies, and my vehicles are raised into the perfection of my Light Body.

I Ascend, in consciousness, into the Kingdom of Heaven, the vibratory Realm of Limitless Physical Perfection...the Realm of my Solar Christ "I Am"!

I stand forth now as a complete God Being within the glorious multi-colored, multi-dimensional radiance of my Solar Christ Presence. My Heart, Mind and Voice are centered within the Twelve-fold Solar Flame of my Solar Christ Presence. My feet are planted firmly on Earth. In this thoughtform, "I Am" a God Being of resplendent Light, now realizing the fullness of that Light on every level of my Being. As "I Am" lifted up, all life is lifted up with me, therefore, I know that within my Solar Christ Presence "I Am" now Humanity standing forth and realizing Her God Being on every realm associated with this Planet. Within my Solar Christ Presence, "I Am" the Cosmic Flame of Harmony, liberating Divine Solar Light into every physical/chemical interaction within my vehicles, healing and restoring all the energy bonds *between atoms* and *within atoms* to the Solar vibration/frequency of Christ Perfection. Likewise, within my Solar Christ Presence, "I Am" this Divine Light of God liberated in every interaction within Humanity and all the energy bonds therein...which include the relationships of all people, organizations, races, religions and nations...liberating these interactions into the harmony of a Higher Order of Being, expanding the Sphere of Humanity's Solar Christ Presence on Earth.

"I Am" experiencing now the Realms of Light Eternal. I visualize and feel the magnificent Solar Archangels stationed at the Twelve Cardinal Points around my Solar Christ Presence. My Twelve-fold Solar Flame radiates out in a great spiral of Love and Praise for these Glorious Agents of the Throne of God. My deepest Gratitude pours forth for Their interest in my personal Solar evolution. On the return current, I feel the entire electronic Forcefield of Light of my Father-Mother God now radiating in a unique Divine Alchemy inward toward the Flame at the center of my Solar Christ Presence. All the Divine Qualities and intent of the Twelve Solar Aspects of Deity are blazing through my Heart Flame out into the world. I feel this as a mighty ocean of Cosmic Lightwaves and High Energy particles charged with the full Causal Body of my Father-Mother God, swirling through a single point—my Heart Flame! I know, with all the faith of my precious God Self, that contained within this flowing electronic pattern of Light is everything necessary to heal my physical body and the entire physical realm...to set straight the orbit, spin and electronic charge of every cell, atom and electron of life on Earth. I feel all Energy bonds within the atomic realm now accelerating in vibration toward the frequency of Limitless Physical Perfection—every cell of life now blazing with full Divine Solar Light.

With the Peace of the Great Solar quiet, I know this Higher Reality within my mind, visualizing it within my glorious Solar Christ Presence, until "I Am" receiving only the Divine Promptings, Ideas and Concepts of my Solar Christ Presence. I feel this Higher Reality within my feeling world, Itself within the great Causal Body of God, until "I Am" a calm ocean of Divine Qualities, blazing forth the Sacred Fire Breath of Holy Spirit awaiting the opportunity to express the Divine Qualities of God into Humanity with every interaction I have. I remember only this Higher Reality in my etheric vehicle, totally enveloped with my Solar Christ Presence, until I reclaim all the memories of the Causal Body of God and remember only the truth of Limitless Physical Perfection. I experience this Higher Reality now within my physical body, and in this visualization, I stand completely within my radiant Solar Christ Presence *in the physical realm!*...until "I Am" a living, Lightfilled Temple of indestructible Perfect Health, Radiant Beauty, Eternal Youth, Vitality and Joy...a Solar Fire Light Body of Christ Consciousness now made manifest on Earth.

For this is the Divine Plan of all "I Am" designed to be as a

Son or Daughter of the Father-Mother God...a Sun of the Sun *while "I Am" embodied on Earth.* This is all Humanity was designed to be as a Race of "I Am" Beings, manifesting and enjoying the Garden of Eden within and all around them, creating a Realm of Limitless Physical Perfection found no-where else in the Universe. "I Am" Humanity now experiencing Her Global Solar Christ Presence as a series of Divine Solar Light interactions, of all Her component parts, until the result is a glorious Global harmony within which all Humanity thrives to Her full God potential. "I Am" Earth's full Spiritual Freedom.

On every *inbreath* through the open Stargate of my Heart, I assimilate my Solar Christ Presence of harmony into all of the Fourth Dimensional space within my vehicles. On every *outbreath,* I radiate my Solar Christ Presence outward, expanding the borders of Limitless Physical Perfection. I have become the Sun, the constant rhythm of *inbreath* and *outbreath,* the source of Divine Life on Earth.

I visualize my Solar Christ Presence now sealing every aspect of my Being. I now experience this around every chakra, organ, cell, molecule, atom and electron of my Being, until all my component parts have each become a Sun unto themself. "I Am" the fullness of My Father-Mother God on every level of my Being.

I again visualize this for the Earth. "I Am" Humanity's Twelve-fold Solar Heart Flame at the center of Her Solar Christ Presence, inbreathing and expanding the glorious perfection of the Infinite Electronic Causal Body of Humanity's collective "I Am" Presence! The Earth now outpictures Herself as a Glorious Sun Being and again takes Her place in the firmament of Heaven as a Star of Spiritual Freedom. Fully accepting this Reality, "I Am" the Earth inbreathed into the Sun, *as a Sun,* the God Victorious fulfillment of the present Cosmic Moment.

Within my Solar Christ Presence, I now come into my maturity as a God Being. As a Child of God, I lived passively in the embrace of my Parents, assimilating Their Blessings laid before me. Now, "I Am" actively co-Creating my own Universe of Perfection in the same sacred process as do my God Parents. Within my Solar Christ Presence, everything in the Universe is to express *as a Sun,* not just within the Sun!...every Planet, every Being, every Atom! "I Am" a Sun, within a Sun, within a Sun...into Infinity.

Now, as the Solar Christ Presence made manifest on Earth, I consecrate my four Earthly vehicles and the four Earthly vehicles of all Humanity.

THE CEREMONY OF CONSECRATION

"I, the Solar Christ Presence of Humanity, do now Invoke, Focus, Expand, Project and Sustain the Sacred Ray of Consecration into the four Earthly vehicles of every man, woman and child. Beloved Ones, feel now this Ray entering your Being as I consecrate your present embodiment to perfect service with the Cosmic Christ. I place my fiery hands of Light upon your Heart, consecrating your feeling nature to the Holy Spirit and every expression of harmony and Love Divine. I bless your mind, consecrating your thoughts to Divine Discernment and God Illumination. I bless your Throat Center and lips, consecrating your voice to speaking only truth, moving the ethers with the sacred sounds of the Godhead. I bless your hands, consecrating your soft touch to the healing and blessing of all life. I bless your feet, consecrating your foundation to staying on the Path of Light throughout this embodiment. I consecrate your eyes to see only perfection, your ears to hear perfection in all things. I bless your nostrils so that you might breathe the Holy Breath of God and seek only the Fragrance of God in all things and in all people. I place my hand upon your Third Eye, consecrating it to reveal to you your Divine Plan every waking moment. I blaze My Flame into each of your physical chakras, consecrating them into complete alignment in Solar Vibration with the Twelve-fold Spine of your "I Am" Presence. I consecrate your physical, etheric, mental and emotional vehicles as a Temple of Limitless Light and Physical Perfection, with the radiation of the Twelve-fold Solar Heart Flame of your Solar Christ Presence and the Infinite Causal Body of God visible and tangible to all life around you. And, I consecrate your Heart Center, allowing it to gently and safely open. Within a forcefield of invincible protection, the Stargate of your Heart is returned to Its original Divine Intent, an open portal for the full manifestation of Divinity on Earth. Through you, I instantly expand this service to a Planetary scale, as I consecrate all of Humanity as the Body of the Solar Christ Presence now returned to Earth.

I bless you with the full consecration of our Father-Mother God, anchoring it physically through you into all Humanity, expanding it forever in eternal service to the Light, until this sweet Earth is wholly Ascended and Free."

And now as your Solar Christ Presence takes full command of your four lower bodies, affirm with deep feeling...

"I Am" a limitless presence of God Perfection.

"I Am" the hand of God now made manifest in the World of Form.

"I Am" Limitless Physical Perfection, Abundance, Joy, Happiness, Love, Illumination, Freedom, Liberty, Victory and God Essence. (Pause...)

"I Am" the Divine Mother Principle of Love now made manifest in the World of Form.

"I Am" the Divine Father Principle of Power now made manifest in the World of Form.

"I Am" the Divine Son/Daughter Principle of Wisdom, the Solar Christ Presence now made manifest in the World of Form. (Pause...)

I now visualize the full Power of my Solar Christ Presence coursing through me. It draws upon my Infinite Causal Body and assists me in formulating my Perfect Divine Response (inner and outer) to every situation. It carries the Reality of *timelessness, spacelessness and Limitless Physical Perfection* in the Eternal Moment of Now. In order to accept this, I allow my Solar Christ Presence to loosen and cut away the bonds that have tied my own personal life to *any* aspect of limitation or fear. I use and use the Transmuting Power within the Sacred Violet Fire. *I Invoke and Invoke all Aspects of my own Solar Being!* "I Am" becoming the potential Sun God or Goddess I truly Am, in Action on Earth. Humanity is now a Race of "I Am" Beings living in a Garden of Limitless Physical Perfection.

"I Am" the Spirit of Transformation!!!
"I Am" the Mother God..."I Am" Love in Action!!!
"I Am" the Father God..."I Am" Power in Action!!!
"I Am" the Son or Daughter of God,
the Solar Christ Presence!!!
"I Am" Wisdom in Action!!!

Through the Power of the 12 x 12
"I Am" that "I Am".

It is done! So be it!

"I Am". "I Am". "I Am".

A MISSION ENDS

I have shared with you the information I received regarding my Earthly mother's transition into the Light, but I want to assure you that her mission on Earth was not unique. We are truly in glorious times, and each and every one of you has volunteered to be part of the incredible birthing process for this Sweet Earth. You have a special thread to weave into the overall plan and your contribution is just as critical and significant as anyone else's.

As you tap into the newly returned energies of the Divine Mother Essence, you will awaken within your Heart all you have ever known or experienced regarding the beauty of mothers or motherhood. Feel the joy of this newly healed aspect of yourself, and be FREE!

As the blessed energies of our Father-Mother God are being balanced on Earth, we are beginning to feel, from the depths of our being, the nurturing Mother's Love that is flowing through our Heart. As this occurs, we are unified with the exquisite energy of our Earthly Mothers. The following poem is a beautiful expression of that Motherly Love as it echos through time. It was written by my beloved friend, Mary Engel.

DIVINE MOTHER

I am an arc in time.

Ancient mothers fill the baskets that I hold, and swing across
a firmament of unmarked skies to the farthest
reaches of my Earth time,
where you stand,
and I thrust the basket into your reluctant arms.

I see your eyes upon the distant mountain,
Vistas of your path illumined by Aquarian Moon,
the path where first I set your baby feet and whispered through
your starry dreams of New Worlds I know,
but may not find.

You are the future as once was I,
And so were those who went before me too,
Who filled their little scan
with women's hopes, with scars of many knowings.
They pass along their treasured dishes, crystal vases, bowls,
triumphant gifts to mark their celebrations,
to set enthroned on ecru lace
in polished wood and beveled glass.

LISTEN!
Trays of gold rimmed glasses--beer and ginger ale and welcome ices
tinkle mid the cricket sounds
and white rose fragrances of a summer night.
Soft exclaiming voices blend with
creaking porch swings
behind the hallmark of Wisteria,
half lit by lamp and half by moon.

Ladies, ladies sitting, hoping, waiting and remembering,
holding essence in themselves,
watching gates along the way, and cousins entering
and porch lights flickering among the leaves.
Horses and carriages along the cobblestones bring
papas home and doctors, priests, and morning milk and
other things.

They drift back into flags and wars and sigh for
stalwarts who marched away to righteous drumbeats
to fight the last war ever--
Again, and then again, and yet again,
They still half listen for their returning steps.

Ladies mark their calendars...confessions, ice man
comes, coal delivered, pump goes dry, gas lights
changed, telephones installed, births and passings.

Memories fade, they peer back into faces neatly set in
musty covered books.
Ah yes, they are here, the many mothers.
Whose eyes are these? Whose brow? Whose stance does
manifest the secret genes we carry filed
within our mortal frames?

Look at those hands, trained to ephemeral pleasures of piano
and of violin, but too, the fashioning of towels and quilts and
lacy forms, enduring stuff that ladies keep about that speaks
their love, their care.
Into all the movements of the aging wrists they weave
the colors and the codings of their days.
Baby fingers, making horserein on their tiny spools,
cross stitch into the intricacies they now weave into their
enduring works, wisdom of continuity and knowing and
remembrance of wickered gardens, green awninged summer
days of flowered tea parties and expectant hush and awe
of baby showers, of grandiose home weddings and of
rainy afternoons with giggling schoolgirls pouring
lemonade and making fudge--of taffy pulls--
Of Christmas lists and wraps and glitter, of joyous bright
decked pine and holly wreaths or solemn white and violet
crepes upon the carved oak front hall doors,
of clotheslines strung with proud embroidered cotton,

of gleaming silver on lacy mats on aristocratic damask.

Pride and passion in days that were a prelude and finale
set in one.

Woolen socks from tiny snow-cold feet, their darned
patches little lumps of ice
thawing into blanketed cushions stuffed into wide oven door,
small fingers clasping steamy cups of broth,
snow babies, swaddled in patchwork cocoons, drift off to
naps and icicles and Jack Frost dreams.

They grew before these mirrors and set their treasured
rings and pins in ribboned boxes in drawers of polished wood
that Papa made, colognes and calling cards and bordered
notes upon the marbled surfaces.
Hatpins, hairpins waiting in their porcelain dishes.
Morning Sunlight through white organdy, church bells and
fresh flowers sent by swains and gracefully placed before
Our Lady, as with all of life.

Crystal rosaries and sweet bisque angel faces. Prayer books
aburst with holy cards to witness morn and evening prayers.
Feather beds and feathering quilts and pillows long and soft.
Kitchen smells of coffee and of kuchen. Alsatian onions
and potatoes and hearty soups and Sunday lamb
and Christmas chicken. Bread toasted on coal stoves
and apple dumplings. Garden mint and nameless wondrous
herbs that comforted and healed.

Through it all, the breeze that spoke of home beyond,
that fondled lace in the bay windows and carried
lily of the valley angel whispers through the rooms,
the breeze that came as household devas traced
the family nest.

Ancient mothers, somehow virgins all, those who birthed
and those who held the threads of timeless Love and
sought their places and nurtured all.
What matters who brought forth the child? It is our line,
and all we carried on, we pass. We give our names, our
blessings, our woven ties. Through us you know of
daily strengths, of gracious ways. We are your island,
your Avalon in the turbulence of now.

And so, their baskets fill with things.
Women, ancient mothers speak through things—their touch,
their understanding fortitude locked in substance. So when
The Earthly form has faded and the face within the frame
wakes no sighs of recognition -- their artistry created
still endures -- locked in every stitch and loop
their Love they pass to you.
So I bring this basket now from far beyond,
from all those fading faces that you never knew.
One day I shall be one of them.
No matter that,
I know of finer fields to sow, my weavings of the mind
and Heart,
A mission ends to pass along the roots,
and so I do,
What shall be now, I leave to you.

I ask you to join me as I celebrate, with my family, the Joy
of my Beloved Mother's newfound
FREEDOM

Elvira Parker Dunlap began her Earthly sojourn on
July 22, 1912,
and she attained her glorious transition into the Light on
December 2, 1993.

DUNLAP, Elvira Parker "Bobbi," made her transition into the
Light on December 2, 1993, while visiting her daughter, Pam,
in Albuquerque, NM. She was 81 years old. She was preceded
into the Light by her husband, William I. Dunlap; and she is
survived by her daughter Pamela D. Earnest (Jim), grandsons,
Tim and Randy and great-grandson Mark of Albuquerque, NM;
by daughter Patricia Diane Cota-Robles (Dickie), grandchildren
Joao and Victoria and great-grandsons Dylan and Hayden of
Tucson; by son William I. Dunlap, Jr. (Becky), grandchildren
Mara, Wesley and Summer of Australia; by son James R.
Dunlap (Nancy), grandchildren Dana and Jacob and great-
granddaughter Caitlyn of Tucson; and by three sisters out of
state. Elvira moved to Tucson with her husband in 1943. She
taught elementary school for 30 years and was a member of the
Retired Teachers Association. She was also a Pi Beta Phi
alumna and an active member of Tucson Women's Club. A
memorial service was held on December 11, 1993, to celebrate
the joy of her newfound Freedom. A memorial fund has been
established in the name of Elvira Parker Dunlap through the
non-profit organization, the New Age Study of Humanity's
Purpose, to assist in supporting free seminars to bring the Divine
Wisdom and Knowledge of God from the Realms of Illumined
Truth to all who seek answers during these challenging times of
change.

We found the following poem with my mother's final papers.
We thought it was a special gift.

MISS ME - BUT LET ME GO

When I come to the end of the road
and the Sun has set for me,
I want no rites in a gloom filled room.
Why cry for a soul set free!
Miss me a little - but not too long
and not with your head bowed low!
Remember the Love that we still share.
Miss Me, but Let Me Go,
For this is a journey we all must take,
and each must go alone.
It's all a part of the Master's plan,
a step on the road to home.
When you are lonely and sick of heart,
go to the friends we know,
And bury your sorrows in doing good deeds.
Miss Me, but Let Me Go.

Author Unknown

HEALING THE ILLUSION OF DEATH
MEDITATION

We are now going to take a journey in projected consciousness into the Realms of Illumined Truth. Please sit comfortably
in your chair with your arms and legs uncrossed and your spine
as straight as possible. Gently rest your hands in your lap with
your palms facing upwards.

Breathe in deeply, and as you exhale, feel all of the feelings
of sadness and grief being lifted away. Breathe in deeply again,
and feel yourself going within to the secret place of the most
High Living God that continually pulsates in your Heart.

As you focus on your own Divinity, as a child of God, feel
yourself being filled with the Love and Harmony of God.

As this Divine Essence begins to fill your Being, every
electron of your physical body is accelerated, and you feel
yourself being lifted up into the embrace of your Higher Self,
your true God Reality.

Your physical body becomes filled with Light. It is shining
and invincible. Every fiber of your Being becomes Lighter, and
you feel yourself Ascending up out of the oppressive limitation
of this physical plane.

Your confusion, doubt and fear begin to drop away, and you
experience a new level of clarity and understanding.

As you are lifted up in consciousness into the Realms of
Illumined Truth, you experience a new, deeper awareness of the
reality of life. You begin to remember that life is eternal, and this
Earth plane is merely a schoolroom of learning. You see clearly
that the belief you had about Earth being the only reality is an
illusion. You see and understand that you are a multi-dimensional Being of Light, and of all the dimensions you abide in, this
physical plane is actually the least real of all.

As you awaken to this truth, more knowledge from the
Divine Mind of God flows into your consiousness, and you are
lifted higher and now higher, until you experience yourself fully

present in the Pure Land of Boundless Splendor and Infinite Light. This is the plane of existence that you will go to when your work on Earth is finished.

As you experience this wonderful Octave of Light, more knowledge flows into your consciousness, and you begin to know the truth of who you are. In this Realm of Truth, you don't just believe or hope, but you absolutely know that you are a child of God. You perceive clearly that when your work on Earth is finished, you will Ascend into this higher frequency of Peace and Harmony.

In this awakened state of consciousness, you realize your Loved Ones who have left the Earth plane before you are very real and tangibly present in this higher dimension of existence. You also know that in this dimension all you have to do is think of them, and through your telepathic Heart communication, your Loved Ones are instantly magnetized to you.

We focus now on our Mother God. We see Her luminous Presence before us. She is VIBRANT AND RADIANTLY BEAUTIFUL. She is filled with the Bliss, the Wonder, the Ecstasy and Awe of Her newfound Freedom. We experience Her Presence with abounding joy for Her happiness on Her return to Earth. We now know that She is always as close as our thoughts. We send Her our Love and our joy, and She embraces each of us in Her Love.

As a special gift to each of us, our Mother God magnetizes to us all of our Loved Ones who have made their transition into the Light, and we see the resplendent presence of all of our family and friends who are now abiding in this higher Octave of Truth.

We send forth our Love to embrace these precious souls, and on the return current, they respond with their Love and joy.

Through the Power of this Love, we are all lifted higher, and we begin to truly know that all life is interrelated. We are all One.

Through this new level of understanding, we consecrate ourself to fulfilling our Divine Plan—our purpose and reason for being.

We join in consciousness with the Divine Love of our Mother God and all of our friends and Loved Ones in the Realms of Light. And as one breath, one heartbeat, one voice, one consciousness of pure Divine Love, we re-dedicate ourself to the fulfillment of our mission on Earth.

Now, through the power of this Love blazing through our Heart Center, we are each lifted up into greater recognition of our purpose and reason for being. And we begin to know deep within...

I came into this world with a very specific purpose. I came to fulfill a mission. I came to Love life and realize the truth about me.

I came to contribute to the salvation of this world. "I Am" a part of God, and the fullness of God dwells in me.

In the mind of God, no one or no thing is useless or meaningless.

Everyone and everything is of critical importance to the balance and order of the Universe.

Without me, God would not be complete. Without me, the Universe would lose its equilibrium.

All that is before me to do I do with happiness and enthusiasm. Nothing is too insignificant.

Never again will there be a sense of futility in my life.

"I Am" overflowing with gratitude to my Father-Mother

God for the opportunity to be in physical form at this time.

"I Am" so thankful to be right where "I Am" right now, serving all who come my way with Love, Joy, Understanding and Forgiveness.

Recognizing my true worth, I now go forth with uplifted vision. I see with my inner eye the Loving and Prospering activity of the Presence of God pulsating in my Heart.

I see with my physical eyes, lavish abundance everywhere.

"I Am" peaceful, powerful and poised, for I know who "I Am".

I have come to Love life free,
and through the activity of my daily life...

SO I SHALL!

A PRAYER OF LOVE

Oh, Supreme Presence of God within all life...
into your Eternal Heart of Love do I immerse myself
now and forever.
I consciously surrender my Earthly vehicle to be merged with
the Love Nature of Your Being until "I Am" a pure focus of
Love...a living jewel in Your Crown of Adoration.

The path I walk in life leads only to Love.
My physical body, filled with Love becomes shining and
invincible.
My Etheric Vehicle, radiating Love, Transmutes the past.
Love in my mind ensures the expression of
Your Divine Thoughts.
Love in my feelings reaffirms that God is
the only power acting.
As "I Am" thinking, feeling and remembering only Love,
I know that God is now working through me...radiating forth
the children of Love: Peace, Contentment, Tenderness,
Happiness, Security, Joy and Opulence...to all
life which I have promised to Love free.

In this awakened consciousness of Love,
my spirit becomes Holy Spirit,
and "I Am" the Love of God reaching out to claim Its own!
In Love, I magnetize all God's Blessings to me,
and in Love, I radiate these Blessings forth to all life around
me. "I Am" the Spirit of Love permeating form until all
is drawn back into the indivisible whole.

I feel the pulsebeat of Love in all life and the continuity of
Love in all experiences I have ever known. It is all Love.
I was born out of Love. "I Am" evolving through Love,
and "I Am" now Ascending back into Love.
"I Am" all Love, and "I Am" grateful.
I Love you, and "I Am" with you always!

CHAPTER THREE

LEARNING TO LOVE YOURSELF

It is an immutable natural Law that in order for us to be capable of Loving any other part of life—any person, place, condition or thing—WE MUST FIRST LOVE OURSELF. In my perception, the overwhelming, underlying factor in every failure, every challenge, every painful experience we are enduring is a deep-seated, ingrained belief of unworthiness and low self-esteem. Most of us on many levels do not feel valuable or deserving of the joy of life. We may intellectually desire it, but deep inside we don't really believe we will ever experience it.

It is time for us to release these distorted beliefs, these lies about ourself we have fabricated, which prevent us from reaching our highest potential and block our natural God-given heritage of happiness, prosperity, health, loving relationships, fulfilling jobs and abounding joy.

As we move forward into the Realms of Illumined Truth, we are perceiving with greater clarity just how these distorted belief systems about ourself were formed. There are several factors involved, and as we truly begin to understand them, we will willingly and gladly let go of our erroneous concepts and accept our reality as Sons and Daughters of God.

Our life, at any given moment, is a reflection of our behavior patterns: our thoughts, words, actions, feelings and beliefs. We are always a sum total of everything we have ever experienced since our inception. As we sojourn through life's challenges, we accumulate a variety of emotions and feelings. Each of us has, at one time or another, undergone the gamut of emotions from bliss to despair. When these emotions are named—happiness, love, comfort, joy or anger, pain, humiliation, rejection, etc., we can often recall the incident and the person whom we consider responsible for evoking such feelings in our life. We can easily remember because the occurrence is recorded clearly in our Etheric Body where it continually pulsates at a subconscious level.

Our Etheric Body is one of the most important, but probably the least understood, of our four lower bodies. It is known as the "seat of all memory," and all of our experiences are recorded within the etheric substance of this vehicle. The Etheric Body is an energy field that interpenetrates every cell and organ of our Physical Body, and it extends a little beyond our body's perimeter. It is comprised of various chemical ethers, and the radiance of this vehicle is often referred to as the aura. Every thought, word, action or feeling we send forth passes through the Etheric Body on an electromagnetic current of energy very similar to a television or radio wave. The frequency of vibration of each current of energy is recorded in the very sensitive chemical ethers of this vehicle.

The records and memories of everything we have ever experienced resonate at a subconscious level in our Etheric Body, and as we sojourn through life, our day-to-day activities periodically activate these memories and bring them to the surface of our conscious mind. It is important that we clearly understand this process because it will reveal to us how our previous experiences and attitudes keep interjecting themselves into our present life situations, confusing the present issues, thus keeping us stuck in the past and preventing us from moving forward.

As an example, when we are born, we are very self-centered, and from our perception as an infant, we believe the world revolves around us. Babies are like little sponges, and they absorb everything that is going on in their environment. They are constantly forming opinions about what the world is like, according to the way they are treated. If they are Loved and nurtured, they observe the world to be safe and friendly. If babies are abused and neglected, they observe the world to be hostile and cruel. Each day children go through a multitude of emotions and feelings, and each and every one of these feelings is recorded in the Etheric Body. As this process continues day after day, the accumulated experiences begin to form a pattern.

For instance, if a child is continually abused, s/he will interpret that experience according to his/her wisdom and understanding at the time of the incident. From a child's frame of mind, adults appear "all knowing" and rather God-like. Consequently, if an adult is abusing the child, the child will think that there must be something very wrong with him/herself. He believes that s/he is bad, no good, worthless. These feelings are very painful, and they leave a powerful vibration of worthlessness in the child's Etheric Body. As the abused child continues his/her journey through life, s/he may experience other situations that s/he interprets as rejection, failure or an indication of his/her lack of value as a human being. As these feelings pass through his/her Etheric Body, they amplify the vibrations of worthlessness recorded there and gradually, day in and day out, as these destructive, distorted beliefs build in momentum, the child starts forming a sense of identity and begins accepting these erroneous concepts as truth. This self-destructive belief of worthlessness becomes an ingrained pattern, and the child then begins to behave in a manner that will confirm his/her belief system.

Whatever we believe about ourself at a deep inner level, we will continually manifest in our life. If we believe we are worthless, no matter what opportunities are presented to us in the way of successful education, Loving relationships, fulfilling jobs, etc., we will find a way to sabotage ourself and fail, because to succeed would be in conflict with who we believe we are. Once we accept an identity, regardless of how distorted it may be, we hold on to it for dear life because the *fear* of finding out who we really are is too great.

If we will each think back as far as we can remember and just observe, in a detached manner, the number of times we didn't feel good about ourself, we can easily see how our low self-esteem was formed. Even children raised in fairly harmonious family situations have all kinds of distorted programming because children don't always interpret situations accurately. We all have records of past hurt, resentment, anger, fear, jealousy, doubt, pain and sadness. We have memories of things that made us feel bad about ourself, not valuable, unimportant—experiences that robbed us of our dignity, our self-respect, our self-esteem. As we reflect over our past, it is easy for us to see that we all have extensive misqualified feelings and thoughts recorded in our etheric memories. Now, as adults, we can review our past and with greater awareness, perceive the error of our childhood perception. We can intellectualize that our abuser was wrong or that the situation did not mean we were "no good" or worthless, but that mental activity doesn't do anything to change the vibrations or the patterns and beliefs recorded in our Etheric Body.

Therefore, through sheer mindforce, we can convince ourself for awhile that we are "okay," but as soon as a difficult circumstance challenges our confidence, those old records are activated, and our failure consciousness of unworthiness is catapulted forth onto the present situation. We thus travel through life dragging the excess baggage of our past with us. We hold onto the distorted belief patterns of who we think we are and proceed to magnetize people and situations into our life who will confirm for us our belief that we are not valuable or worthy. This vicious circle has been a normal mode of operation for literally centuries. It is a behavior pattern that must cease.

In order for us to be truly FREE to fulfill our Divine Plan, our purpose and reason for being, we must Transmute our distorted concepts and accept the reality of our God Self. In truth, all feelings of low self-esteem, unworthiness, failure, loneliness, rejection, etc., are nothing more than separation from God. When we lift up and reunite with the Presence of God, all feelings of unworthiness drop away. Low self-esteem cannot be sustained in the Presence of God's abundant Light.

Our relationships are mirror reflections of our consciousness. Whether they are wonderful or destructive or a combination of both, at any given moment, they are reflecting what we are sending out through our thoughts, words, actions, feelings and beliefs. I know this is one of the most difficult concepts to accept, but as we learn more about the complexity of our Being, we begin to clearly perceive the truth of that statement.

We live, move and breathe within an electromagnetic forcefield of energy. Daily, this forcefield is created and sustained by our thoughts, attitudes, emotions, actions, frame of mind, beliefs, etc. All four of our lower bodies contribute to this forcefield that surrounds us: physical, etheric, mental and emotional. This electromagnetic forcefield is just as the name implies—MAGNETIC. Consequently, it magnetizes energy to itself that is vibrating at the same frequency.

Every single person on the Planet is evolving within their own self-created electromagnetic forcefield. Once we understand this reality, it makes it easier for us to recognize how our relationships reflect our consciousness. For example, if we are suffering from ingrained beliefs of low self-esteem and unworthiness, those distorted vibrations will fill our forcefield and magnetize to us other people whose forcefields are also vibrating with low self-esteem and unworthiness. When our forcefield enters the forcefield of the other person, the discordant vibrations are amplified for both of us. This makes us very uncomfortable, and we begin to feel that we don't like each other. We may even argue or attack the other person verbally.

If we are feeling good about ourself and our forcefield is filled with Love, we will magnetize to ourself someone who is also content with who they are. As we enter each other's forcefield, these positive feelings are amplified, and we feel very comfortable in each other's presence.

Now, in these two examples, I have greatly simplified the process, but that is the essence of what occurs.

We must realize that every person on the Planet has myriad frequencies pulsating in their forcefield from all of their Earthly experiences. Therefore, our relationships are very complex. Sometimes the same person can amplify within us positive and negative frequencies at the same time, thus creating a Love-hate relationship.

The advantage of having this knowledge is that we can now use our relationships as wonderful tools and opportunities for growth. By observing how we feel about the people in our life, we can determine what we are feeling about ourself. Often, we are oblivious to our true feelings. Because life has been so painful, we have numbed ourself as a means of survival. But, now with greater insight, we can observe every facet of our relationships and know that the way we *feel* about each person is reflecting some aspect of ourself.

When someone "pushes our buttons," it means they are amplifying a frequency in our own energy field that we are not comfortable with. If we didn't have that particular frequency in our forcefield, they could not "push our buttons." I know this is difficult to accept, because when someone is a source of irritation for us, the last thing we want to see is any comparison to ourself in their behavior. But, the only reason people affect us in an adverse way is because, at some level, we are buying into what they are saying or doing. At some level we are believing them even if we are fighting tooth and nail to deny it. If we really didn't believe what they were saying, it wouldn't have the same effect on us.

With this wisdom, we can evaluate all of our relationships: parents, spouses, children, relatives, friends, lovers, co-workers, employers, associates, casual relationships and all of Humanity. We can observe where we are buying into destructive beliefs and where we are giving our power away. Then, we can Transmute our electromagnetic forcefield by reprogramming our self-concept and self-image. As we recognize and accept our true God Reality and release all negative beliefs about ourself, we will see our feelings and attitudes toward our relationships changing miraculously. When our forcefield is filled only with Love, our relationships will reflect that LOVE.

People truly treat us and perceive us the way we perceive ourself. If we don't like the way people are treating us, we need only to Love ourself more, and our relationships will be transformed. Experiment with this truth, and you will create for yourself the Loving relationships you have been desiring.

Naturally, this doesn't mean that every single person we come in contact with will automatically express only Love and Light with every thought and word, but it does mean that we will stop giving our power away to people. When we Love and respect ourself, they will no longer have the ability to affect us in an adverse way simply because we will no longer buy into their behavior or take it personally. We don't have control over the things people say or do, but we have *absolute* control over how we choose to let their words and actions affect us. When we allow people the space to be who they are without allowing them to affect us adversely, we will have truly accomplished the goal of taking our power back. We will Love ourself and amplify the Love in them. Hence, they will be lifted up out of their negative feelings to a degree and gradually, they will begin to believe they are valuable also. This will improve our relationships all the way around.

Occasionally, we may be in a relationship that is abusive or violent. Sometimes we have such a low opinion of ourself that we magnetize someone into our life who will "punish" us in a way we subconsciously feel we deserve to be punished. This is not an uncommon pattern in people who were abused as children. Needless to say, anyone who abuses another person, either physically, mentally or emotionally is not Loving or respecting him/herself. People who are so severely programmed may not be able to start Loving themselves just by experiencing our Love, but as we begin to Love ourself, we will value ourself enough to extricate ourself from abusive situations. We will no longer tolerate violence or abuse of any kind.

Sometimes, the fear of leaving a relationship is greater than the fear of abuse, but I promise you, when you begin Loving yourself, you will magnetize such wonderful people into your life that you will gladly let go of destructive relationships.

I am a counselor, and one of the things I have people do to begin Loving themselves more is to write a list of all of the wonderful qualities they possess. Sometimes people feel so bad about themselves, they cannot come up with even one positive trait. In that case I have them look at all of the people they Love and admire and list the qualities they appreciate in those people. The reality is that our relationships are mirror reflections of ourself. Consequently, for us to even recognize and appreciate particular wonderful qualities in other people means, *at some level*, those qualities resonate as truth within us, regardless of how oblivious we may be to them.

The only reason we believe we are stupid or worthless or failures is because we affirmed those lies to ourself over and over again throughout our lifetime. Now, to reprogram ourself we must begin daily affirming the TRUTH.

It is time now to take that exercise a step further and reach into an even higher level of our potential. Instead of just listing the things we Love and respect about ourself or writing down the things we Love and respect in other people, we need to tap our limitless God-Self. Before beginning your list, quiet yourseg149lf; take time to feel centered and connected with your Heart. Feel the Love of God flowing through the Stargate of your Heart and say to yourself, "If I had no limitations—no time and space limitations, no family limitations, no financial limitations, etc., and I could instantly be the most positive, whole, complete, successful, prosperous, effective Loving human being on Earth, who would I be, and what would I do?" Then, begin writing down the thoughts that flow into your mind. Write them in the present tense beginning each statement with "I Am." Don't feel self-centered or conceited. Don't censure or edit your thoughts; just allow the creative ideas to surge forth. Let go of any nagging thoughts of self-ridicule or self-doubt, and let the vision you are experiencing register in your feelings.

There is an expression that states, "What the mind can conceive, the person can achieve," but the truth is the most glorious, perfect person that you can possibly imagine being in this moment is going to be barely scratching the surface of who you really are and who you are capable of becoming. This list will serve as the blueprint and the beginning thoughtform for the "new you." This will be the new program, the new belief system and the new sense of identity you will start emulating, but it is just the beginning. As you focus on this wonderful vision of yourself, it will grow and evolve.

Remember, whatever you put your attention and energy into, you bring into form. Whoever you *believe* you are, you become. Our thoughts are creative. So, what you are actually doing is creating a new program that you will put into the computer of your brain to reprogram your old patterns of unworthiness and low self-esteem. Your brain really is your computer system and you know the expression in computer talk, "garbage in, garbage out." Well, that is exactly what you have been doing. Now, it's time to remove the old floppy disc with the erroneous program on it, and replace it with a wonderful new floppy disc program. You need to focus on your list everyday, and affirm the truth of your vision with deep feeling. You need to let go of all disbelief, and **ask your God Self to Transmute all resistance, all interference, all blocks, all doubts that are, in any way, preventing you from manifesting the vision of the "new you."** As this vision begins to register in your feelings, as a true identity, you will act out of this new sense of identity, and you will actually *become* your vision.

In the beginning, your vision will just feel like empty words. You'll hear the voice of your lower human ego saying, "Who do you think you're kidding?" But, continue to repeat the affirmations *everyday* anyway. You must "fake it till you make it." Remember, the only reason you have low self-esteem is because you, or other people in your life, affirmed that you were worthless over and over again until it finally began to register as truth, and you eventually accepted that *lie* as a sense of identity. Now you are doing the opposite. You are going to be affirming the TRUTH of your innate value as a Son or Daughter of God with limitless potential, and day-by-day this identity will begin registering as real.

To accelerate the process of removing the old negative program, you must utilize the gift of the precious Violet Flame of Limitless Transmutation. Constantly ask your God Presence to blaze the Violet Fire in, through and around every thought, word, action or feeling you have ever experienced that is in any way preventing you from becoming the reality of your new image. Ask that the cause, core, effect, record and memory of low self-esteem be instantly Transmuted into Light. And, begin to accept and know the truth of who you are.

The following is an *example* to give you an idea of what your list might include, but every person is unique, and only your God Presence can reveal to you your perfect vision and blueprint, so be sure and make your own list.

"I Am" recognizing who "I Am", and I Love and respect myself.

"I Am" continually manifesting wonderful, Loving relationships in my life.

"I Am" expressing Limitless Physical Perfection, slim, firm, flawless form, Eternal Youth, Vibrant Health, Radiant Beauty, perfect eating and drinking habits.

"I Am" Divine respect for my four lower bodies: physical, etheric, mental and emotional.

"I Am" Loving every aspect of myself, including my sexuality.

"I Am" in a fulfilling, creative and financially rewarding job.

"I Am" open and receptive to God's limitless flow of Abundance.

"I Am" an exponent and example of Divine Family Life, including my place in the family of Humanity.

"I Am" expressing my highest potential as a daughter/son, wife/husband, mother/father, grandmother/grandfather, woman/man; friend; relative; co-worker; human being; Earth steward; Lightworker; teacher; example; wayshower and integrator of Heaven and Earth, Angels and Elementals.

"I Am" Divine Happiness, Humor, Laughter, Joy and Fun.

"I Am" Divine Confidence, Self-Esteem, Trust, Integrity, Honesty, Truth, Reverence for all Life, Acceptance, Tolerance and Inner Knowing.

"I Am" Divine thoughts, words, actions and feelings.

"I Am" Divine Illumination, perfect speech, communication, listening, writing and learning.

"I Am" Transfiguration, Limitless Transmutation, Hope, Ascension and every other conceivable Divine Quality of God.

"I Am" the perfect manifestation of my Divine Plan and the Divine Plan of Beloved Mother Earth and all Creation.

"I Am" in constant communication with the Realms of Eternal Truth and the Divine Heart and Mind of God.

"I Am" permanently manifesting, in my daily, tangible life, the perfection of Heaven on Earth.

"I Am" an exponent of Divine Government, human rights, animal rights and Mother Earth's rights and Liberation and Freedom.

"I Am" perpetually held in the embrace of God's invincible Protection, and with every breath I take, "I Am" expanding the borders of the Kingdom of my Father-Mother God.

Learning to Love yourself is a process that will require every bit of your patience, acceptance and tolerance. It will require the full power of your attention and your constant thoughts and feelings. You cannot change a lifetime, probably hundreds of lifetimes, of believing you are worthless, into recognizing you are actually a Divine Being with limitless potential, by just affirming the positive vision of the "new you" for five minutes a day.

We are such creatures of habit that if we aren't consciously focusing on what we want to manifest in our life, and monitoring our thoughts and feelings constantly, in no time, we will fall back into the dysfunctional patterns of self-flagellation. Obviously, if you affirm your value and self-worth for five minutes a day and then beat yourself up for the rest of the day, you're not going to succeed in changing your self-image. Remember, "The price of freedom is eternal vigilance." You must consistently, throughout the day, monitor your thoughts and ask yourself, "What am I thinking and feeling about myself now?...And how about now?...And how about now?" If you aren't feeling good about yourself, you need to *immediately* correct the situation. Say to yourself, "No, that is an old erroneous thought pattern, and it is no longer who 'I Am'. 'I Am' a valuable, Lovable person." Then, think of the list you have written of the "new you," and begin affirming it with deep feeling. Keep the list in your pocket, if you want to, or just take one statement on the list and affirm it over and over again until it starts to *feel* true. Then, affirm the next statement, then the next. Sometimes it helps to visualize yourself walking through Golden Doors, and as the doors close behind you, envision all of the old patterns of low self-esteem are left behind the door. When an old negative thought or feeling pops up, just consciously put it on the other side of the door, in your mind's eye, and flood it with Violet Fire. Affirm that this is part of the past and no longer appropriate for you to think about or feel. Look at what is coming up, and ask yourself, "What do I want to be expressing in my life instead of this old negative belief about myself?" Then focus on what you *want* to be expressing instead of what you *don't want* to be expressing.

Initially, this process feels very uncomfortable. It feels self-obsessive and self-centered. It may even feel egotistical. Normally, people are so used to telling themselves they are worthless that sometimes it even feels like self-deception. But, even in the face of all of this resistance, you must continue the exercises in spite of how uncomfortable you feel. Often, the discomfort is generated by the lower human ego which is fear-based. This aspect of your personality has thrived on your misery and doesn't want to let go of its control. It is actually throwing a temper tantrum to prevent your God Presence from taking full control of your vehicles because it thinks it is going to die if that happens. You must Transmute your human ego with the Violet Flame, and flood it with Love so it will feel safe enough to let go and be transformed.

The next step in learning to Love yourself is taking care of yourself. This change in your behavior will feel even more foreign than the positive affirmations. This step means you have to actually ask yourself in *every* situation, "What is the highest good for me?" That thought normally sends shock waves through people. Imagine the audacity of thinking of yourself *first*. Doesn't that totally conflict with everything you have ever been taught? Well, it conflicts with everything we have all been taught, and that is why we are so co-dependent and dysfunctional.

The important thing to understand about this step is that you are lifting up in consciousness, and you are transcending your lower human ego. Consequently, when you ask, "Is this the highest good for me?", you must ask this question to your God Presence and not your human ego. Your human ego is self-obsessive and operates strictly to gratify your physical senses. It is also based in fear, so when it responds to that question, the answer will always be selfish, greedy and usually at the expense of everybody else. In other words, the "dog-eat-dog," "looking out for number one" syndrome. *But,* when you ask your God Presence that question, that aspect of your Being is always functioning on all levels with regard to the highest good for all concerned. Your God Presence is always prompting you forward to your highest potential, and It clearly knows that this must be accomplished with reverence for all life. It will *never* be true that if you fulfill your highest good, other people or other lifeforms will be hurt in the process. Your Divine Plan just doesn't conflict like that. This means that if you are *truly* doing what is the highest good for you in a particular situation, IT WILL ALSO BE THE HIGHEST GOOD FOR EVERYONE ELSE INVOLVED, even if they don't perceive it that way. It will *never* be the case that if you are fulfilling your Divine Plan, it is preventing someone else from fulfilling their Divine Plan. When there seems to be a real conflict, then you must realize that someone's human ego is involved and not their God Presence.

Another thing you must understand in this step is that you are not helping anyone by being a martyr and sacrificing what is right for you just to make someone else happy. Even if you are giving them what they want, if you have had to sacrifice what is right for you in the process, it is *not* going to be for their highest good. When people make these self-sacrifices, it is because they want to be Loved and approved of; they also want to be accepted. The problem is that you are actually invalidating yourself and negating your value as a human being when you make decisions to try and be what everybody else wants you to be, instead of who you are. For one thing, it is impossible to fulfill everybody's expectations, so you are always disappointing someone. When you try to be what everybody else wants you to be, you become so confused you totally lose touch with who you are and what you are supposed to be doing to fulfill your Divine Plan on Earth. This is really a tragedy that consistently holds you in bondage.

When you are not accomplishing your Divine Purpose and reason for being, no matter what you do, you never feel fulfilled.

You will always feel like something is missing in your life, and you experience dissatisfaction with everything you attempt. This, once again, leads into failure consciousness and low self-esteem. Then the vicious circle begins all over again.

Now, to relieve your fears that you are being selfish to think of yourself first, I want to assure you that your God Presence is the most Loving, caring, understanding, compassionate Being you could ever imagine. When this aspect of yourself is making the decisions of what is the highest good for you in a situation, you will be receiving ideas on ways to Love, heal, help, benefit and nurture the people involved that you never dreamed of before. **The difference is, your actions will also result in Loving, healing, benefiting and nurturing yourself in the process.** When this transformation in your behavior pattern occurs, you will move out of the "poor me" consciousness. Then, instead of feeling victimized, you will experience the joy and wonder of really being a positive, effective person.

The next step in developing self-Love is learning to nurture and pamper yourself EVERYDAY. When you take the time to really take care of yourself, you transmit the message to the computer of your conscious mind that you are valuable. I know that life is hectic, and people usually use that as the excuse for not taking time to pamper themselves, but you need to recognize that is a cop-out and create a new belief system. Affirm to yourself daily, *"I have all the time I need to accomplish whatever I need to do today, including taking quality time to Love and nurture myself."* I assure you that there is not another "job" that you have to do that is more important or more beneficial than learning to Love yourself. **Every single thing existing in your life is reflecting how you feel about you**—this includes your relationships, your job, your finances, your health, your state of mind, your spirituality—everything. Learning to Love yourself is the most critical and urgent factor in transforming your life. Remember, your life is just reflecting your consciousness. When you go about trying to change the situations in your life without changing your self-image and the way you feel about yourself, it is like trying to change the reflection in the mirror without changing the object that is causing the reflection. It is a futile effort.

Many times the thought of nurturing and pampering oneself is so foreign to people that they can't even imagine what to do. Just begin by asking yourself, "What would make me feel really good right now? A walk in nature? Reading a good book? Taking a bubble bath? Relaxing with a warm cup of tea? Having a massage? Eating something healthy? Meditating? Taking a nap? Playing a game? Making Love? Sharing time with someone I Love? Praying? Communicating with a special friend? Writing my innermost thoughts? Doing my affirmations? Listening to an uplifting tape? Listening to music? Playing music? Interacting in a really fun way with my family?", etc.

The important part of this step is that whatever you choose to nurture yourself must *genuinely* be for you, not just doing what other people want you to do. When you are taking time for the special nurturing and pampering of yourself, consciously acknowledge to yourself that this is what you are doing. Say to yourself, " *'I Am' doing this for me because I Love myself, and 'I Am' worth it. 'I Am' filling myself up with Love and tenderness. This fills me with joy and a sense of fulfillment and happiness.* "

The exciting thing about the new awareness that is pouring forth from the Realms of Illumined Truth is that you don't have to understand it all fully. You don't have to totally accept it or even believe it. All you have to do is experiment with it, and put forth the required effort to change your negative habits. If you do, you will prove it to yourself beyond a shadow of a doubt.

This process of transformation is scientific and accurate to the letter. If you genuinely Love yourself, you will value yourself enough to feel worthy of Loving relationships, prosperity, health, happiness, joy, peace and all of the other gifts that you have been blocking and denying yourself through your low self-esteem. Then, you will feel safe enough to open the Stargate of your Heart and allow God's limitless flow of abundance to pour into your life. You will know and accept, "All that my Father-Mother God has is mine."

CHAPTER
FOUR

TRANSFORMING YOUR RELATIONSHIPS

Through the application of Love, it is possible to transform your relationships with your romantic interest or family members, friends, neighbors, co-workers and associates from sources of tension, anxiety, frustration and often, even anger and hatred, into avenues of Love, harmony, comfort, joy and even peace and serenity. Through self-awareness, you can learn to use your Love and energy as a positive force in your life.

At any given moment, our life situation is a sum total of our thoughts, words, feelings and actions. The electronic energy we continually use to think, move, feel, breathe and live in the physical realm is a gift of life that is given to us by God in a pure and neutral state. As we send this energy forth into the atmosphere, we have the free will to let it pass through us constructively or to intercept that pure energy and misqualify it into discord. What we must always keep in mind is that *we are responsible for that decision.*

This electronic energy is intelligent life. It has a degree of consciousness, and its purpose is to serve life. Once we accept this truth, it will help us to be more responsible about how we use or abuse this energy. What actually takes place is that this electronic substance comes forth from the Universal Source of all life vibrating in an octave of perfection. It is joyous, buoyant energy, eagerly entering its service to life. Every moment of the day we are receiving this energy and charging it with our thoughts and feelings. Depending on our state of mind and emotions, we either receive this life energy and allow it to pass through us in harmony, which is a blessing, or else we misqualify it and send it forth as an inharmonious mutation that causes friction and adds to the chaos on the Planet.

Once the energy has passed through us into the physical realm, it will remain as part of the overall energy of the Earth. There is no way of destroying energy. *All we can do is Transmute the negative energy back into its original vibration by sending positive energy into it.* Since this is the case, the mutations we have sent forth will keep returning to us over and over again until we Transmute them back into positive frequencies. Each time this energy returns, it is greatly magnified over what we originally sent out because of the energy of a like nature that it accumulates along the way.

This energy returns through our normal life experiences. Natural law uses whatever means are available to bring this energy back to us, so that we will have the opportunity to Transmute it into its proper vibration. For instance, it can be brought to us through our interpersonal relationships, our jobs, our health, our daily activities or whatever other vehicle is available.

Once we accept that every experience in our life is natural law, *in kindness,* returning the energy we have sent forth, either to bless us, or to give us the opportunity to Transmute it back into perfection, then we will be able to look at our trials and tribulations as opportunities rather than tragedies.

Regardless of the means natural law uses to return our misqualified energy, whether it is through family problems, problems with other relationships, problems with work, finances, health or whatever, THERE IS NO PERSON, PLACE, CONDITION OR THING THAT CAN INJECT ANYTHING INTO OUR PERSONAL EXPERIENCE WHICH WE HAVE NOT CREATED, IN SOME EXISTENCE, TIME FRAME OR DIMENSION.

I know that is an awesome statement, but it is from the Realm of Illumined Truth.

Every single person on this Planet is special and unique. There are no two people alike. As this electronic energy passes through our Heart Center into the world of form, it is stamped with our own individual electronic pattern. After the energy completes its journey in the world of form, it returns to the Heart Flame pulsating with the *same* electronic pattern. This explains how natural law can determine what energy belongs to whom, and there is no way we can disclaim ownership of the returning energy with our electronic pattern stamped on it.

The very positive side of this law is that since we have created the negative situations in our life, by whatever means, we have the ability to do something about them. Accepting responsibility removes the feeling of injustice or the "poor me" syndrome, and it changes us from the position of being victims of circumstance to the position of being creators of circumstance.

We must realize that this energy returns, not to plague us, but rather to give us the opportunity to change the vibration back to its original frequency. Remember, this is intelligent life energy that we have distorted, and we are responsible for restoring it back to perfection.

Accepting responsibility for our present life situation does not mean resignation or submission to the negative things that are taking place, but rather, it means developing a calm and detached attitude about them, recognizing each situation as an opportunity to Transmute our misqualified energy and literally *Love it free*. When we resent persons, places, conditions and things in our life, it is usually because we have not understood the principle of natural law. Now that we realize we have created our present life situations by misqualifying energy through our thoughts, words, feelings and actions, instead of rebelling when it is brought back to us, we can look at these circumstances as opportunities to Transmute our discordant energy and, in fact, *be grateful*.

The more quickly we learn to Transmute the negative circumstances of our life back into the vibration of harmony through the power of Love, the more quickly our life will be the expression of happiness we are yearning for.

This is not an easy concept to grasp. Because of our lifelong programming, it is common for us to look at the chaos in our life and ask, "Why me?" We may be driving down the street, and someone runs a red light and hits our car. From all outer appearances, we seem to be completely innocent. We may say to ourself, "Of course it's true that I have been judgmental and critical all of my life, but what does that have to do with a car accident?" Our boss may come in and read us the riot act for no apparent reason. Our children may be causing us all kinds of problems. Our relatives and friends may be mean and hateful to us. We may become physically ill. We may lose our job or develop financial trouble of some other nature. We may be miserable in our marriage. We may fall down and break a leg. We may have mental problems and be anxious and confused. We may be robbed. Our house may burn down. We may be involved in a natural disaster of some sort, or any number of other things can go wrong. It is not important to know exactly why these things are happening in our life. We don't have to go back and dig up the past. It is self-defeating to blame or chastise ourself. The only thing that matters is that we acknowledge that somehow, somewhere, sometime, we misqualified this energy, and now, natural law is returning it to us to give us the opportunity to Love it free.

If we can maintain this attitude, it will greatly assist us in dealing with our negative life situations calmly and rationally. If we can truly understand that the persons, places, conditions and things that are being used to bring our misqualified energy back to us are just the instruments or vehicles being used by natural law, this will allow us to be objective about the situation and not tie into it with more anger or resentment.

For instance, if we have a relative or a boss or any other person who is continually causing us problems, we should step back and look at the situation as an objective observer. We should acknowledge that it is not the person's fault. He or she is just the vehicle being used to return our own negative energy to us. The truth is that this is our own energy returning to us, and if this person wasn't bringing it back, someone else would. It's that simple. If we get angry or upset with the person, it only compounds the problem. Then, we have not only the original energy to Transmute but the additional anger as well. This additional anger will then go out from us again, accumulate more negative energy, and somehow it will be brought back to us at another time. As we can see, by responding negatively, we have been creating quite a vicious circle for ourself.

The process of *Transmuting* the trials and tribulations of your life back into vibrations of harmony is accomplished in **four easy steps**. First of all, when negative circumstances occur, accept that this is merely your own misqualified energy returning to you for requalification. *Regardless* of how this energy is returned, when a negative situation occurs, consciously think to yourself, *"This is my own negative energy returning to me. 'I Am' not going to get mad or upset at this person or condition because they are just being used as an instrument to return this energy to me. 'I Am' going to observe the situation objectively. 'I Am' going to remain centered and calm. 'I Am' going to handle this situation in the most constructive way possible, and 'I Am' going to Love this energy back to its original vibration."* The first step is **ACCEPTANCE**.

Then, you must consciously thank the Universe for the *opportunity* that has been provided for you to Transmute this negative energy from discord to harmony. Say to yourself, *"I give thanks to the Universe, and 'I Am' grateful for the opportunity to Love this energy free."* The second step is **GRATITUDE**.

Next, you must consciously ask for forgiveness for misqualifying the energy by saying, *"I ask forgiveness for the misqualification of this precious gift of life. I ask forgiveness for all other life energy I have ever misqualified, both known and unknown, and I forgive myself for misqualifying this energy."* The third step is **FORGIVENESS**. Forgiveness is a frequency of the Violet Flame of Limitless Transmutation. Visualize Violet Light pouring through the Stargate of your Heart into the situation at hand.

Then, consciously send Love into the situation. This is done through creative visualization. The color pink, in all of its hues, carries the vibration of Love. So to send Love into a circumstance, you need to ask the Universal Source of all life to send forth the essence of pure Love. Visualize this pink energy flowing through the Stargate of your Heart; then project this pure pink Love forth from your Heart Center as a mighty laser beam of pink Light into the negative energy returning to you, and say to yourself, " *'I Am' Loving this negative energy free.* " The fourth step is **LOVE**.

This **four-fold activity of Acceptance, Gratitude, Forgiveness and Love** creates an extremely powerful forcefield of constructive energy around you, and as the negative energy enters this forcefield, it is actually raised from a heavy, discordant frequency into a high, harmonious frequency.

This energy is electronic Light substance, and as we increase the frequency of vibration from discord to harmony, it is the same as increasing the voltage of Light in a dark room. Darkness cannot be sustained in the presence of Light. Discord cannot be sustained in the presence of harmony.

Once this negative energy has been Transmuted into positive energy again, it will continually remain a part of your overall constructive energy and magnetize good things into your life.

Through the process of deduction, we can see that if we discipline ourself and gain control of our thoughts, words, actions and feelings so that we are no longer misqualifying energy, and learn to handle the negative circumstances of our life positively and constructively as we Transmute the returning negative energy back into harmony, it will only be a matter of time until we no longer have negative energy returning to us. At that point, our life will truly be transformed into an expression of joy and happiness.

This does not mean that there will no longer be negative things happening on the Planet. Until everyone becomes master of his or her life, negativity will exist. But it means that our own individual world and our experiences will not reflect this negativity. This is known as being *in the world but not of the world.*

Then, through our example, we will be able to help our friends and Loved ones attain peace in their own lives, and this knowledge of self-mastery will gradually be passed fro`m one person to another until this entire Planet is experiencing the Universal Oneness of all Life and living in peace. I know this sounds too good to be true, but it's happening at this very moment, and you are a catalyst. I want to thank you for being here on Earth at this time, and I want to thank you for being you.

Now, let's look more deeply into the power of Love, so that it will really be a practical tool and not just an ephemeral thought.

In recent years, we have heard a great deal about unconditional Love. Because of misunderstandings and half-truths, there has been a lot of "bad press" on this subject. I would like to state clearly that unconditional Love does *not* mean allowing yourself to be a subservient, abused doormat, and it does *not* mean that you should remain in a destructive relationship no matter what.

Unconditional Love means allowing another person to be who they are and appreciating their uniqueness rather than demanding that they conform to your expectations.

At the present time, most people allow themselves to Love another person conditionally. They agree to Love someone on the condition that the person looks the way they want them to or has the "right" religious beliefs, the "right" skin color, the "right" nationality, the "right" job, the "right" social standing, the "right" political affiliations and on and on.

All of this kind of Love is crooked, and through it, we are cheating ourself out of some of the most rewarding, fulfilling friendships imaginable.

The more we discover about this electronic energy that makes up all life, the more we become aware that what affects one part of life affects all life. This electronic Light permeates every part of life in the Universe; consequently, we cannot have a negative thought without adding to the negative vibration of energy for the entire Universe. What *affects one, affects all.*

Einstein spent his entire life trying to prove the Unified Field Theory, the interrelationship of all life—in actuality, the *Oneness of all Life*. If you will just contemplate that point for a moment, you will be able to see with a greater awareness how absolutely absurd it is to be prejudiced or to discriminate against any other part of life. To say you hate someone because of their race, religion, gender, nationality or anything else, is like saying you hate your hand, or you hate your arm, or you hate your leg. They are actually *part of you,* and you cannot hurt them without hurting yourself. What a different place this Planet will be when this truth finally registers in the consciousness of every man, woman and child living here.

We all know that there are many people participating in very objectionable behavior. Unconditional Love does not mean that we should condone or support their destructive behavior, but it means that we should handle the destructive behavior in a constructive way and search for the positive characteristics in their personality and accentuate them. We should not hate these people, reject them, humiliate them or cast them aside to go out and do something else destructive. Whatever we put our attention and energy into, we intensify; therefore, it is imperative that we learn to only intensify the positive behavior in another person.

From my observation, I think people demonstrate unconditional Love most consistently with their children. Occasionally children do some really terrible things. Parents feel it is their responsibility to handle the situation, so they do, sometimes more calmly and constructively than others, but they do their best, according to their wisdom. Then, they rebuild the child's sense of self-worth by pointing out the good qualities the child has to offer. Parents realize that these children are part of them and, therefore, how they behave is a reflection on them. So instead of just casting them aside and hating them or never speaking to them again, the parents strive to the best of their ability to help the children correct their problems and become constructive, worthwhile human beings.

This is the exact same attitude we need to develop toward everyone. If we will just realize that all people are a part of us, then we will be able to relate to them from a better perspective. We will be operating from a position of *how can I help this part of myself,* rather than from a position of hate and rejection.

The best thing to do is to be a radiating example of unconditional Love. The only way we ever teach anyone anything is through example. We can expound on the principle of Love until we're blue in the face, but unless we are living, tangible proof of that law, all of our words will be to no avail.

First, we need to consciously create a forcefield of Love around ourself by drawing forth the vibrations of *Acceptance, Gratitude, Forgiveness and Love.* This is accomplished by simply asking our Higher Self to enfold us in this four-fold activity. Then, we must **feel** ourself being enveloped in the radiance of Acceptance, Gratitude, Forgiveness and Love as these Divine qualities flow through the Stargate of our Heart. This forcefield has to be deliberately maintained. If we call it forth and then have a temper tantrum, we shatter our forcefield, so we need to Transmute the negative tantrum, and, then, re-establish our forcefield of Love again.

The more proficient we become at sustaining this forcefield of Love, the more harmonious our life will be. When we are centered and balanced within this forcefield of Love, we will be protected from tying into negative situations with our anger or frustration. The more efficient we become at this, the more calmly and effectively we will be able to deal with our spouse, lover, children, relatives, friends, co-workers, bosses and associates. Rather than trying to function through the blinding eyes of emotion, we will be able to stand outside of the storm and operate as an objective observer.

This takes a great deal of discipline and practice, but it

works. Each day that we practice this Law of Love we will become more efficient, and soon it will be a natural part of our behavioral pattern.

By changing the way we respond to the people in our life, we can transform the entire relationship. It is very difficult to stay angry or continue to be nasty to someone when they are remaining calm and responding with Love. We have probably all experienced a situation in which we were extremely angry, and we may have even been ranting and raving at someone. If they remained calm and Loving, we realized after a short time that we were making a fool of ourself.

We must accept that everyone has the right to be who they are; there is nothing we can do to *make* another person change. All we can do is change our own responses. But, almost miraculously, when we begin responding with Love, the relationship will change from a source of tension or anger to a source of calm and peace.

Love is magnetic and also contagious. Remember that the power of Love raises the discordant energy of hate, anger, frustration, anxiety, tension or any other destructive emotion into a more harmonious vibration. So, if we are radiating out enough Love, we can actually change the atmosphere around us. This is not wishful thinking. This is a scientific natural law, and it is well worth our every effort to attain the discipline of Love. We can be *channels* for Love by opening the Stargate of our Heart and by expanding our forcefield of Love to engulf our home, office, neighborhood, city, state, country and Planet.

In striving toward more harmonious relationships, one thing we must realize is that each and every person on the Planet is going through the specific learning experiences that s/he personally needs for his/her own development and growth. Contrary to outer appearances or our opinions, *all people are doing the very best they can with their life, according to their understanding of the law.* Outer appearances are often very deceiving, and we never know just why another person is going through a particular life experience or behaving in a certain way. We must develop tolerance and patience in dealing with other people and, whenever possible, reveal to them the Law of the Circle (whatever we are sending out expands and returns to us), so that, with a better understanding, they will take the steps necessary to get their life in order. This does not mean preaching or interfering in any way with another person's free will. It merely means being in tune with all life and, when the opportunity arises, to help another—*give them a drink from your cup.*

In reference to specific circumstances in our relationships, it is almost always possible to maintain harmony as long as we refuse to respond with anger, but there are occasions when another person insists on depriving us of our rights by abusing us physically, emotionally or mentally. We are never obliged to remain in an abusive situation. The best thing for us to do is to remove ourself from the situation, and send Love and forgiveness into that energy from a distance.

It is also possible to communicate with the Higher Self of that person. Our Higher Self is actually our super-conscious mind, and this consciousness can be reached through the process of thought. We can actually speak to the Higher Self of another person with telepathic communication. All we have to do is think of the name of the person, and then ask the Higher Self of that person to take command and intervene on the destructive behavior, and fill the person with illumination, wisdom and understanding, so as to eradicate the self-defeating behavior according to the Divine Plan of the individual.

This telepathic communication can be done at any time with our relationship. But remember: our Higher Self operates only from the Octaves of Perfection, so don't ever try to manipulate anyone through this method. Our Higher Self will only work to help us reach our highest potential.

In my counseling, I have found that by changing responses, a person can usually rekindle the Love that was once in a marriage and restore the relationship to happiness. But occasionally, after much effort and discipline, one may become aware that, even though one partner is maintaining an atmosphere of Love and harmony, the spouse is not adding to the joy of the marriage, but is just existing. One then comes to a point of re-evaluation. A lack of friction is not everything in life. If it is obvious that one partner is putting 98 percent into a marriage and the spouse is putting in only two percent, it may be time to step back and determine if this is what is really wanted. Is this enough? Some people will say as long as they are living harmoniously and not fighting, it is enough. Others will say they want more sharing, a more fulfilling relationship and decide this is not enough. This is a very individual choice, and each person should have the freedom to decide for him/herself.

I would like to point out again *that what we put our attention on, we intensify and draw into our life.* If we dwell on a particular personality trait, attitude, or behavior in another person that we find objectionable or offensive, we are actually compounding the problem and making it worse. The more we practice self-control and become a radiating center of Love and peace, no matter where we are, the more cognizant we will be that our friends and loved ones are emulating more peace and calm in their behavior as well. It is possible to raise the awareness of all those around us by raising our own consciousness. Once we become the masters of Love, we will reap tremendous rewards. We will realize that by responding with anger, resentment, frustration and hatred, we have been giving our power away and allowing other people to manipulate our emotions and control our life.

With our newfound mastery of Love, we will be able to interrelate with others much more effectively. We will be able to communicate rationally and share our thoughts and feelings. We will be able to recognize the choices in our relationships and make intelligent decisions. We will be more receptive and able to release and let go of misconceptions. We will be more willing to compromise, and we will realize that two working together can draw perfection into this world much more quickly than one. We will ultimately experience happiness as a state of well-being that we can attain only by taking charge of our life.

We have come to the point in the evolution of this Planet when it is not enough just to be harmless. It is not enough to be negatively good, which means just ceasing to do wrong. It is time for us to put forth our energy into deliberately improving the quality of life, not only for ourself, but for the rest of Humanity as well.

The sea of energy we are living in permeates all life on this Planet. With our every thought, word, action or feeling, we are adding either to the Light of the world or to the darkness. As has been said before, *we are either part of the problem or part of the solution.* Let's be part of the solution.

By creating a forcefield of Acceptance, Gratitude, Forgiveness and Love, you can magnetize to yourself a life of happiness and fulfillment. Our opportunity is at hand, and the time is NOW.

CHAPTER
FIVE

COMMUNICATING WITH
AN OPEN HEART

We communicate in a myriad of different ways, but our clearest message is always the example of our own behavior. For instance, when a child observes his parents doing something in a particular way, the child believes that is the way it should be done. If a child sees his parents continually responding with self-discipline, restraint, dignity, harmony and the ability to maintain order in their own lives, then the child will come to accept that is the correct way to live.

The key quality to effective communication is LOVE. Ultimately, Love is everything. When we Love something, it is of value to us, and when we value something, we spend time with it; we enjoy it, and we take care of it.

TIME is another very important factor in effective communication. When we devote time to our relationships, even when it is not demanded by glaring problems, we will perceive in them subtle needs for improvement.

We can easily make the necessary changes in ourself and share with the other person our perception of the problem. Often, with gentle urging, administered with thoughtfulness and care, minor corrections and adjustments can be made that will make what seemed like a great problem melt into nothingness.

The *quality of time* we devote to our relationships indicates to the other person how much we value them. We can repeatedly profess our Love to another person verbally and mechanically, but if we fail to devote significant, high quality time to the relationship, our profession of Love will be perceived as hollow and empty. Again, our behavior is the greatest communicator.

When we truly LOVE people, we value them. When we spend quality TIME with them, we transmit the message that they are VALUABLE. The feeling of being VALUABLE is the foundation of our sense of self-worth and high self-esteem. The feeling of being valuable is also the cornerstone of self-discipline because, when we consider ourself valuable, we will take care of ourself in all of the necessary ways.

Self-discipline is self-caring, which results in high self-esteem, and high self-esteem paves the road to success and fulfillment.

We can expand our communication skills by learning to quiet ourself and asking our Higher Self for guidance and illumination regarding a particular relationship or situation. There are many things our Higher Self will reveal to us when we take the time to ask and listen. We will learn things such as:

"I Am" not a victim of circumstance. "I Am" a creator of circumstance.

I have a purpose and reason for being.

The people I come in contact with in my life are there for a reason. Whether the relationship is intimate or casual, each interaction is an opportunity for learning and growth.

No one knows what another person's learning experience is. Consequently, I do not always know what is best for another person.

In other words—what is true for me may not always be true for the other person.

It's okay for me to share my perspective and opinion in a situation. It's also okay for the other person to perceive things differently than I do.

This doesn't necessarily mean that one of us is right and the other wrong. It merely means that we each have a different perspective according to our wisdom and experience.

It does not diminish my value or self-worth if another person disagrees with me.

The greatest gift I can give another person is the freedom to experience the lessons life is presenting according to his/her own Divine Plan.

I now realize that only my Higher Self can guide me unerringly to my highest potential, and I now know this is also true of every man, woman and child on Earth.

I believe the majority of our problems in communication result when we try to project our belief system onto a situation and then ASSUME the people involved are believing and experiencing the same thing we are.

For instance, when I counsel couples, I first see each of them separately to hear their individual perception of what is occurring in the relationship. Usually, it's hard to believe they are involved in the same relationship because they are each seeing things so differently. Each one is assuming the other person is seeing things just like they are, and therein lies the problem.

For example, she may say, "He doesn't Love me because he's not affectionate." In reality, what she means is, if she wasn't affectionate, it would be because she didn't Love him. Instead of just projecting her feelings onto him, she needs to find out what *he* means when he's not affectionate. When the subject comes up in a joint session, he is often shocked that she even felt he wasn't affectionate in the first place. From his perspective, he may feel that he was being affectionate, and he might not understand at all what she means. It is clear that we need to stop playing the game of "mind reader," and we need to stop assuming our partner is a "mind reader" too. We need to really get in touch with what our needs are in the relationship. Then, in a Loving way, we must communicate those needs to our partner. This should not be stated as an ultimatum but rather as a positive request to enhance the quality of the relationship for both of you. Then, ask your partner to really evaluate what his/

her needs are in the relationship, and ask him/her to share with you how s/he feels you might add to the improvement of the relationship.

It's important for both of you to listen to each other's needs with a Loving, open Heart and an attitude of cooperation. If your partner's requests feel like you are having to become somebody else in order to be what s/he wants you to be, then you need to re-evaluate the situation. This process of communication doesn't mean co-dependency. We should not have to sacrifice who we are just to be what someone else wants us to be. If that is really the case, then it is the wrong relationship.

Our relationships are, however, opportunities for us to stretch and grow. Usually, our partner's needs do not negate who we are or demand that we be someone else; they just encourage us to reach deeper into who we are and expand and enhance the qualities we need to develop anyway. As we let go of our defensiveness and the need to always be validated by our partner's approval, we will be able to hear their needs in a different Light. We will not hear their requests as criticism or judgment, but rather we will hear them as what they really are: *their needs*. This will help us to be more receptive and responsive instead of taking it personally and feeling like we are inadequate or failures. We will not feel attacked, so we won't feel like we must respond with defiance and anger. This will immeasurably improve the relationship, and it will enable us to start trusting enough to keep our Heart open. We won't close down out of fear or feel too vulnerable to share our true feelings. This means of communication will feel safe and comfortable. As we take time to have meaningful conversations with each other *DAILY*, our trust will increase, our Love and understanding will deepen, and we will develop our ability to listen and really hear what our partner is thinking and feeling without being threatened.

In our very busy life, these intimate moments of communication don't just spontaneously happen. We need to deliberately schedule time to talk to each other *everyday* without interruptions. This doesn't have to be for a long time, but it must be consistently everyday. It is far better to share 15 minutes of Loving thoughts everyday than to spend two hours one day and nothing for the rest of the week.

These special times of communication are specifically for the purpose of keeping you connected with your partner on a Heart level. It is a time to share Loving feelings, happy thoughts, hopes and dreams. It should be fun, fulfilling, productive, intimate and rewarding for both of you. This is not a time to solve problems or discuss issues. Make time separately for your trouble-shooting sessions. You will find that when you have consistently connected and opened your Heart to your partner on a daily basis, the problem-solving sessions will be infinitely smoother. Our desire to cooperate is greatly enhanced when we are speaking with someone we are feeling Loving toward instead of someone we've been fighting with all week. The genuine feeling of wanting to add to the joy of our partner's life motivates us in a very positive way. The mood of cooperation is reciprocal, and as we keep the Stargate of our Heart open, our Love for each other will grow day-by-day in a very wonderful way.

When we realize that each and every person has a very unique life experience, we understand that no two people see things quite the same way. By the time we're adults, we have been through all kinds of experiences and we have molded them into our perception of what is real and true. Consequently, when two people are going through a situation or challenge, they are each seeing things very differently, depending on how they have experienced life. What is more important, however, is that they are each *SUPPOSED to see things differently because they are*

each learning something different from the situation.

No two people are going through the exact same learning experience. Therefore, it is interference for us to try and *force* anyone to see things our way. We do that when we are feeling insecure or trying to validate ourself by having others agree with us. It is perfectly all right for us to share our perception of what is going on in a particular situation, but it is not okay or even appropriate for us to tell someone else their perception is wrong and demand that they see things our way.

Again, the need to be "right" and have people agree with us will dissipate when we begin reprogramming our sense of identity with high self-esteem. Then, our methods of communication will be greatly improved. Instead of saying, "This is the way it is, and you're wrong," we will be able to say, "This is the way I feel when you behave in a particular way. This is what is going on for me in this relationship. What's going on for you? What are you feeling when you behave in that particular way?" We will then be able to learn a great deal about our relationships. We will also be able to let go of judgment, criticism, condemnation and fear.

Communication means to transmit information or feelings. We must evaluate our attitudes and see if we are really communicating or just trying to force our beliefs and perceptions on others. A slight adjustment in awareness can turn each interaction into a truly fulfilling HEART CONNECTION and not just another battle to make people see things our way, so that we can feel secure in our beliefs and validated in our perceptions.

In a relationship, you need to allow yourself the space to form your own opinions and develop your own perceptions. It is okay for you to be who you are, and it's okay for you to have your own opinions. It doesn't matter if there isn't another person on the Planet who sees things in exactly your way. That is the beauty of your uniqueness. But, in a relationship, it usually doesn't work very well if we are always acting out of diametrically opposed beliefs and perceptions. Consequently, we need to really listen to each other and say, *"I understand how you are feeling, and I hear what you are saying."* You may not be able to relate to your partner's perception, but you don't need to. All you need to do is listen. Then say, *"We've both shared our perspective of what is going on in this situation, and we have very different opinions of what should be done. Let's do some brain-storming and see if we can't come up with a solution or idea that we both feel comfortable with."* Probably 98 percent of the time you both, coming from a Loving place, will be able to come up with a compromise that you feel good about. On rare occasions you may just have to *agree to disagree.* In those instances, the more secure you are about yourself, the more easily you will be able to just "let go and let God." Loving, open communication based in honesty and integrity is the key to deep, meaningful relationships. It is the avenue through which we really get to know and understand our partner, and it is a powerful tool that will allow us to rebuild our trust, heal our pain and open our Heart more quickly or effectively.

CHAPTER
SIX

HEALING THE PAIN OF BETRAYAL

There is probably not another Earthly experience that creates deeper, longer-lasting wounds than when someone betrays our Love. Even though we can intellectually say to ourself, *"We are all going through the learning experience we are supposed to be going through, and at some level I have agreed to go through this experience or I wouldn't be in this situation,"* that normally doesn't relieve the intensity of our pain.

Betrayal of Love can occur at any point in our life, and it can be perpetrated upon us by anyone we deeply Love. Parents can betray their children's Love by abusing them or neglecting them. This betrayal can cause deep-seated problems that often affect the child adversely for the rest of his/her life. Since we are always a sum total of everything we have ever experienced, abused children, as adults, usually continue the pattern of having their Love betrayed by magnetizing dysfunctional relationships into their lives again and again.

When we begin developing romantic relationships, we draw people into our life who treat us and perceive us the way we feel about ourself. If we have a past embroiled with self-loathing, failure consciousness, unworthiness and low self-esteem, we will magnetize people to us who will fulfill our belief system by treating us like dirt. In addition to this extremely negative situation, there are myriad lesser degrees of self-flagellation that are consistently being reflected in our relationships.

Betrayal of Love can manifest in a multitude of ways from physical violence to verbal and emotional abuse; drug and alcohol abuse; infidelity; abandonment; rejection; neglect, etc. The pain inflicted on the betrayer's partner is excruciating, and from all outer appearances, seems unbearable. It's true that people can do and say what they want, and it can't affect us adversely unless we allow it to, but when we have opened our Heart to someone in Love and trust, it is incredibly difficult not to experience pain when that Love and trust are betrayed.

Unfortunately, when that happens, we learn to protect ourself by closing down our Heart with the hope that if we don't allow ourself to Love, we won't ever have to experience that kind of pain again. Needless to say, that is a tragedy that also prevents us from experiencing the bliss of Love again.

The good news is that we are awakening to the truth of our human potential. We are understanding with greater clarity how life in this physical plane really works, and we are discovering that, contrary to what we have previously believed, we are *not a victim;* we are creating our own reality. What this deeper awareness means is that we have a *choice*. At any given moment our life is reflecting who we believe ourself to be. This includes our relationships, our financial status, our health, our career and every other facet of our life. If we don't like what our life is expressing, then we need to change our belief system and change the way we perceive ourself. We need to heal our wounds and create a new sense of identity that reflects the Loving, positive, successful, effective person we are capable of being.

Healing the pain of betrayal is a process, and it is a very important part of changing our self-image. We cannot feel good about ourself and create an attitude of high self-esteem with gaping wounds from the past still throbbing with pain.

To begin the process of healing, we must Transmute the frequencies of agony, grief, sadness, loneliness, despair, anxiety, shock, hopelessness, fear, anger, etc., that we suffered when we became aware of our betrayal. Eighty percent of our energy is released through our Emotional Body, our feelings, so you can just imagine the wreck our Emotional Body is in after we have gone through such a horrendous experience. Remember, every thought, word, action and feeling passes through us on an electromagnetic current of energy similar to a radio or television wave. This current of energy is recorded in our Etheric Body and continues to reverberate in the energy field around us. If the frequency of the energy is positive, that's great, but if it is negative, then we are creating a serious problem for ourself.

When we experience betrayal, our pain becomes all-consuming. We dwell on, and even obsess about, what has happened. This creates a heavy, dark cloud of oppressive energy around us. If we could see, with our inner vision, the energy field we are creating, we would clearly recognize the gravity of the situation. The feelings of hurt and pain are often so distorted that they appear in our energy field like black pockets of sticky tar. This distorted energy interpenetrates every fiber of our being and causes all manner of havoc. It actually blocks the Light from reaching us, so during the time when we need the Love and comfort of God the most, we render ourself inaccessible.

This energy field around us is also magnetic, so it magnetizes to us other energy vibrating at the same frequency. This has the effect of amplifying what we are feeling, so we sink deeper and deeper into the quagmire of misery. In order to stop this downward spiral into oblivion, we must Transmute the negative energy we have projected into our energy field. There is no destroying energy. We can't just start thinking and feeling positively. Positive thoughts and feelings are always good, but if we don't Transmute the negative energy back into Light, our positive thoughts and feelings will just begin forming a forcefield of Light *around* the black tar-like substance, and we will still be subject to all of the negative impact of our pain. With this understanding we can see just how imperative it is for us to Transmute our negative thoughts and feelings, as well as changing the way we are thinking and feeling.

During this unique time on Earth, we are receiving unprecedented assistance from on High to enable us to Transmute the negativity of our past and present existence. The gift from God that will incalculably assist us in this healing process is the Violet Flame of Limitless Transmutation. Due to the major shifts in vibration that have occurred on Earth recently, we are capable of withstanding greater frequencies of this Holy Light than ever before. This Sacred Substance is actually an activity of Divine Alchemy. As we invoke the Violet Flame of Limitless

Transmutation from the very Heart of God and ask our God Self to project It into the negative thoughts and feelings surrounding us, this Sacred Fire actually flows into every electron of negativity in our forcefield, and It begins accelerating the vibration of the energy. This causes every atom, molecule, electron and sub-atomic particle to spin more rapidly on its axis. The centrifugal force of this activity throws the black tar-like substance off of the particles of energy and Transmutes It back Into Light. As we continue the use of this Violet Flame day after day, the negativity in our energy field is dissipated and Transmuted back into Light. This has the effect of lifting us up out of the agonizing grip of pain into the harmony and balance of healing.

This process doesn't wipe our memory away, so we will still remember what we have been through, but it *removes* the emotional charge of pain. This allows us to be neutral about our experience, and when we get to that point, our healing is complete.

The following exercise is a very simple, but very powerful tool to heal the pain of betrayal. Use this visualization daily until you feel your healing is complete.

VISUALIZATION

Begin by sitting comfortably in your chair with your arms and legs uncrossed. Breathe in deeply and allow all of the stress or thoughts of the day to just drop away. This is a very special time for you, so *be here now.*

Feel yourself going within to the Golden Throne room of your Heart, the secret place of the most High Living God. There you kneel before the altar of Love and surrender the consciousness of your lower human ego to the perfection of your true God Self. Now, sit upon the Golden Throne, and become aware that all of your Earthly vehicles are being brought into perfect alignment. Your physical, etheric, mental and emotional bodies are integrating perfectly with your God Self, and you are being lifted up into the Realms of Illumined Truth. From this octave of Enlightenment you know and understand that you are within an invincible forcefield of Eternal Peace, and you know you have the ability to Transmute the pain of your past and present effortlessly.

Now, invoke the Light of God that is ALWAYS Victorious...

In the Name of the Almighty Presence of God "I Am" and through the full power of the Divine Spark pulsating in my Heart, I invoke now, from the very Heart of God, the most intensified activity of the Violet Flame of Limitless Transmutation "I Am" capable of withstanding. I ask my God Self to project this Divine Substance into every electron of precious life energy I have ever misqualified in any time frame or dimension, both known and unknown, since I was first breathed forth from the core of Creation. (Pause...)

"I Am" experiencing the Sacred Violet Fire blazing through the Stargate of my Heart into every person, place, condition or thing in my life. I command, through the power of God pulsating in my Heart, that every thought, word, action or feeling I have ever expressed that is less than God's Perfection, be instantly Transmuted back into Light. I command that all negativity that has ever passed between me and the relationships in my life be instantly Transmuted into Light. I command that the residue of all pain or suffering I have ever caused or experienced be instantly Transmuted into Light. (Pause...)

Through the Divine Alchemy of the Violet Flame of

Limitless Transmutation, "I Am" Healed; "I Am" Restored; "I Am" Rejuvenated and "I Am" Transformed into the perfection of my true God Reality.

*Now, through the Presence of God "I Am", I invoke the full-gathered momentum of the Sacred Fire of Divine Love, and I ask my God Self to project this Holy Substance into every electron of precious life energy that has just been Transmuted into Light. The pink essence of Divine Love **permanently** seals this healed energy in an invincible forcefield of Love, so that it will never again be distorted into a frequency that is less than God's Perfection.*

I accept that this Divine Activity of Light has been accomplished with full Power, to be increased daily and hourly with every breath I take until "I Am" wholly Ascended and Free.

It is done. So be it.
"I Am"

CHAPTER
SEVEN

WHY ARE WE SO CO-DEPENDENT?

The word co-dependent has become a common term in the field of psychology to describe our dysfunctional behavior patterns that are usually based in low self-esteem. Co-dependency means that we validate ourself by trying to be what other people want us to be. This is usually done at the expense of ourself. A co-dependent person is consistently striving for approval and acceptance by sacrificing his/her own needs to fulfill everyone else's expectations. Normally, this behavior is counter-productive to everyone involved. It often cripples the person we are co-dependent with because it prevents them from being self-sufficient and capable. Instead, it encourages them to be dependent and ineffective in managing their own life. This is called "enabling," and it perpetuates dysfunctional behavior patterns in all of our relationships.

Co-dependency is cropping up in so many diagnoses that people are amazed at how prevalent it is. But, the truth is, we have all been raised to be co-dependent from the time we were born.

From the moment we can first understand, our parents are guiding us and telling us what to do and how to behave. This is an important part of our learning experience, but the problem is that through this process, we clearly get the message that if we do what we are told and do what is expected of us, then we are "good little girls/boys," and if we don't, we are "bad." Children are like little sponges, and they learn very quickly what they need to do to get acceptance and approval.

It is only recently that we have begun to discover how critically important it is to empower our children to develop a sense of high self-esteem *simultaneously* as we guide them. We used to believe that if we praised children too much or let them make their own choices, they were going to become self-centered, conceited, egomaniacs. Now, we know that it is actually quite the contrary. When we honor our children and encourage them to get in touch with who they are and encourage them to think for themselves and make good decisions and choices, they develop a level of self-respect and confidence that will serve them in a positive way for the rest of their lives. When we are constantly correcting them and focusing on what they are doing wrong and then telling them how they should think and feel, they develop an attitude of inadequacy, and they lose trust and self-confidence in themselves.

I have taught several workshops in prisons, and the inmates there reflect the extreme of what happens when we don't honor and empower our children. The inmates I work with have usually been through hellacious childhood experiences. Through their abuse, they developed an identity of worthlessness; then as adults they acted out of that belief system and did terrible things to prove that they were worthless. That was not always a conscious decision, but we act out of our belief systems, and we become who we *believe* we are.

To avoid developing co-dependent behavior patterns in our children, and to correct our own co-dependent behavior patterns, we need to tap the reality of our God Presence and recognize who we are. Then, we need to assist our children in realizing how special they are also. We must remember that we are ALL glorious Beings who have come to Earth to experience this third dimensional school of learning. We each have a unique plan, and we have brought with us, encoded in our Divine Blueprint, all of the knowledge and skill we need to bring that plan to fruition. No one outside of our God Presence knows just exactly what our plan is or how to fulfill it. Therefore, when we are always trying to be who everybody else thinks we should be, we are creating chaos and confusion in our life. We are actually blocking ourself from reaching our highest potential.

It is time that we take our power back and start outpicturing who we really are. Self-empowerment automatically transcends co-dependency. It is impossible for us to be empowered with our God Self and be co-dependent at the same time. As we allow our

God Presence to integrate with our four lower bodies and once again take full dominion of our thoughts, words, actions and feelings, co-dependency will become a malady of the past.

CHAPTER EIGHT

MAKING PEACE WITH YOUR SEXUALITY

Sexuality is a beautiful expression of Love. It is an intimate, sacred communion between two people. When experienced with an open Heart, it can transcend the limitation of physical reality and allow one to soar into the octaves of ecstasy, wonder and awe; it can lift our Heart; it can nurture and heal; it can fill our very Being with peace and contentment, and it can expand our capacity to Love.

Sexuality is a very important part of our Earthly school of learning. But, unfortunately, like so many other things, it has been misunderstood, distorted and abused. Now, during the Cosmic Moment of Beloved Mother Earth's rebirth, this aspect of our Being must be healed, purified and Loved so that it, too, can Ascend into the Fourth Dimensional Octaves of Perfection.

We are Ascending into the Light *physically*. That means the Ascension of our four lower bodies, as well as the Ascension of the Earth Herself. For this to occur in Divine Order, every facet of our Being must be Loved free from the entrapment of our lower human ego. This includes our sexuality. We cannot just suppress it and deny that it exists. We need to lift our sexual experience up out of the quagmire of depravity into the embrace of our Solar Christ Presence, where we will know the joy and elation of its original Divine intent.

It seems as though we have created the same confused attitude about sex that we created about money. Interestingly, sex and money are the two things that our lower human ego uses most effectively to keep us stuck in negativity.

For aeons of time, the monetary system of the world has been abused. Instead of the natural exchange of give and take, based on the principle of always working toward the highest good for all concerned, the wealth of the world has been used by the elite few to manipulate, dominate, oppress and control the multitudes.

Money has been such a source of pain and suffering through-

184 Stargate of the Heart

out history that religious orders in both Eastern and Western cultures considered money itself to be innately evil. They, thereby, denounced it and actually took vows of poverty. This action gave the Spiritual aspirants of the world the message that somehow poverty was a virtue. This belief system perpetuated the schism between the haves and the have nots. It also created a phenomenon that intensified the abuse of money because the people who were truly seeking greater levels of truth to improve the quality of life on the Planet and those who genuinely were striving toward spiritual growth and self-mastery were being taught by the world religions that money was evil and should not be acquired. That belief left the money in the hands of those who were not pursuing the highest good for all, but rather were pursuing the self-indulgent gratification of greed and power.

If we observe what has transpired on the Planet as a result of the abuse of our sexuality, we will witness the same thing. For aeons of time, sex also has been used to manipulate, dominate, oppress and control people. It has fallen to the depths of abuse and degradation. As this condition developed, the religions of the World began to distance themselves from this physical experience. In order to encourage their followers to do the same, they initiated all kinds of taboos regarding sex. They took vows of celibacy and proclaimed chastity a virtue. This created quite a quandary. Each soul knew and understood that through the sacred communion of sex, one of the most miraculous events on Earth occurs, which is the procreation of life. On the other hand, we were being told by religious leaders that sex was "bad." These two diametrically opposed concepts could not be effectively reconciled in our finite minds, so we learned to muddle through life vacillating between wanting very much to fulfill our sexual experience and beating ourself up with guilt and shame if we did. This was a coup de grace for our human ego, because our confusion created a very powerful vehicle through which our human ego could manipulate us and keep us bound in self-abuse.

Remember, the human ego is an aspect of our personality that developed as we used our free will and our creative faculties of thought and feeling to create thoughtforms and experiences on Earth that were conflicting with God's Will. As we fell into denser and denser frequencies of vibration, our connection with our Holy Christ Self was short-circuited. Eventually our human ego developed to the point that it was able to take control of our physical, etheric, mental and emotional bodies. This aspect of our consciousness began manipulating our four lower bodies for its own selfish intent. The human ego obtained a sense of pleasure from physical sensations, so it focused its attention on physical gratification. Our sexuality is our most sensual experience, so this area of our life became dominated by our human ego. Consequently, our ego prompted us to fulfill our sexual pleasure obsessively and often abusively. The human ego has no concept of integrity or moral conscience, so as we progressed through our Earthly sojourn, our sexuality deteriorated from the sacred communion it was intended to be into a compulsive addiction. People striving to attain self-mastery believed that the only way to break this "bad habit" was to stop doing it. But, because sexuality is an important part of our learning experience on Earth, the desire for it never went away. Forced celibacy usually resulted in different degrees of frustration, anxiety and even sexual perversion. Sexual suppression was registered in our consciousness as self-deprivation, so we began negating our self-worth and abusing ourself in other ways as well. The denial of sexual expression manifested as compulsive behavior patterns in other areas such as eating disorders, substance abuse and self-loathing. It caused us to suppress our feeling nature, and we numbed ourself, so we wouldn't be tempted. As we closed our Heart Center, we experienced loneliness, rejection, isolation and many other grossly mutated forms of self-flagellation. The human ego, aggressively rebelling against the attempted suppression of our sexuality, intensified its efforts to force us into expressing ourself sexually. The ramifications of that rebellion resulted in sexual abuse and all manner of sexual perversion. It also resulted in lesser degrees of negative sexual expression, such as promiscuity and infidelity. This sad scenario has been acted out on the Planet now for millennia. It is such a common part of our everyday experience that, to this day, sex is considered just a "dirty" thing that we do, and it is considered part of our downfall. Rarely is sex ever thought of as an avenue for our Spiritual growth.

Needless to say, if we are in the process of physically Ascending into the Fourth Dimension, we can't just deny part of who we are and pretend it doesn't exist. We also can't eliminate our sexuality by Transmuting it into Light, so it will go away, the way we do other forms of misqualified energy. Our sexuality is part of who we are, and instead of getting rid of it, we need to make peace with it, and we need to learn how to express it positively and constructively. We need to recognize it for what it was intended to be, an expression of Love. And we need to Love ourself enough, so that we will allow wonderful relationships into our life through which our sexuality can be experienced in its highest level of potential.

Because of the pain people have experienced in past sexual relationships, there is a tremendous fear associated with the process of daring to open up and trust again. Sometimes the lack of trust involves other people; sometimes we just don't trust ourself. The truth is we have all been through the gamut of sexual experiences, either in this lifetime or other lifetimes. Because of the negative influence and power our human ego has inflicted on us in this area of our life, I don't believe anyone has passed through the Earth plane unscathed by the sexual experience. And we all have the accumulated sum total of these experiences clearly recorded in our Etheric Body. These frequencies of sexual abuse, dysfunction, guilt, shame, fear, etc., continually pulsate at a subconscious level into our daily life. This subliminal influence is one of the main causes of our inability to open up to positive relationships. It is imperative that these negative experiences of the past be Transmuted into Light before we can ever hope to create new, positive experiences.

If we can just envision all of our past as a program on a "floppy disc" in the computer of our mind, it makes perfect sense that if we don't take out the old "floppy disc" before we put a new disc with the new program into our computer, we will just have a garbled mess.

Once again, the most effective and most powerful tool we can use to remove the old "floppy disc" is the Violet Flame of Limitless Transmutation. This sacred substance can be used *without fear*. Many times people have been sexually abused as children and have blocked all memory of the incident from their mind as a coping mechanism. The Violet Flame will not bring things up and force us to remember. It will just enter the etheric records and Transmute them cause, core, effect, record and memory back into Light.

The key to Transmutation is *consistency*. We need to invoke the sacred Violet Fire *daily*, and we need to feel It blazing in, through and around every electron of our Being *perpetually*.

INVOCATION

In the Name of the Almighty Presence of God, "I Am" and through the full power of God pulsating in my Heart, I invoke now the most intensified activity of the Violet Flame of Limitless Transmutation "I Am" capable of withstanding at this moment. Blessed Flame, blaze in, through and around every electron of precious life energy I have ever misqualified that is associated with my sexuality. Transmute instantly the cause, core, effect, record and memory of every negative sexual experience I have ever had, both known and unknown, from any time frame, dimension or existence back to my inception. (Pause...)

*I ask that this activity of the Violet Flame be maintained, increased daily and hourly, moment by moment, the maximum that Cosmic Law will allow, until "I Am" wholly Ascended and **Free!!!***

What I ask for myself, I ask for every man, woman and child evolving on Earth.

I accept this done with full Power.

So be it.

Beloved "I Am".

While we are in the ongoing *daily* process of Transmuting our past negative sexual experiences, we can simultaneously begin creating a wonderful new "program" for our computer.

Because of the shifts in vibration and consciousness that have taken place on the Planet over the last several years, we are in a more optimum place than ever before to, once and for all, heal our sexuality and return that aspect of our Earthly experience to the dominion and authority of our Solar Christ Presence.

Prior to reconnecting with our Solar Christ Presence and the Twelve-fold Solar Spine of our God Presence, we were very much restricted to our Planetary vehicles and our Seven-fold Planetary Chakra System. When our communication system with our God Self became short-circuited and we lost contact with the Realms of Illumined Truth, we tried to figure out, with our limited finite mind, just how our creative faculties worked. We saw that, initially, the creative life force was released through the three lower chakras. This enabled us to procreate and bring forth life. But, we believed with our distorted perception, that in order for us to express our creativity through our higher chakras (Heart, Throat, Third Eye and Crown), the life force had to be raised up out of the lower chakras into the higher chakras. We perceived this to be the raising of the

Kundalini in a way that actually took the creative life force out of the lower chakras and transferred it into the four higher chakras. When neophytes were beginning the process of self-mastery, they believed that if they expressed themselves sexually, the creative life force was drawn back down out of the higher chakras into the lower chakras, and they believed that this delayed their Spiritual growth. That is why celibacy became an intricate part of the training for self-mastery.

Now, with the merging that has taken place between our Seven-fold Planetary Spine and our Twelve-fold Solar Spine, we have new insight and a deeper understanding as to how the creative life force flows through our spinal column. This Divine Light that sustains us in the physical plane enters the top of our head through the Crown Chakra, and It descends down into our Heart Center. This Light is then directed into the Root Chakra at the base of our spine by our Holy Christ Self. The Light activates the Root Chakra according to our individual Divine Plan; then It begins Its ascent up the spine into the Crown Chakra, awakening each chakra along the way according to our highest good. The Creative Life Force flows to us from the Heart of God, and It is, therefore, limitless. For us to think we have to take the life force from the lower chakras in order to have sufficient life force to activate the higher chakras is a mistake. In truth, we have been blocking our progress by suppressing and denying our sexuality, instead of promoting our growth as we thought we were doing by being celibate. So, now is the time when we need to reach higher and higher into the Realms of Illumined Truth and tap the wisdom and knowledge pouring forth from the Divine Mind of God that will set us free from the fear and confusion of our sexuality. If we invoke the God Qualities of Divine Discerning Intelligence, Reason and Common Sense into our life, we will begin to see how we have been deceiving ourself and how ludicrous our attitude about sex has been. We will recognize that the confusion, fear and taboos we have established around sexuality are really based in ignorance and the manipulation of our lower human ego. Remember, the ego has a lot to gain by keeping us entrapped in guilt and shame. It's impossible to become an empowered Son or Daughter of God when you are filled with self-loathing. As long as we are beating ourself up and feeling worthless, the human ego has full reign of our four lower bodies.

Instead of trying to correct all of the erroneous beliefs and taboos we have about sex, why don't we just visualize ourself walking through Golden Doors, passing from the old consciousness of the human ego into the Solar Consciousness of our Christ Presence. The doors close behind us, and we *know* that the distortion and misinformation of the past is no longer part of our reality. We see that the Violet Flame of Limitless Transmutation is blazing through all of the experiences we have left behind, and we are like a glowing blank piece of paper on which our Solar Christ Presence will reflect the *truth* of our sexuality.

The first step in awakening to the Divine Intent of our sexuality is learning to Love and actually revere our physical body. This vehicle is a miraculous living organism that allows us the opportunity to experience a third dimensional reality. It is the vehicle that our Holy Christ Self must use to project the creative faculties of thought and feeling into the physical plane. Without a physical body we could not become co-Creators with God or masters of energy, vibration and consciousness in a physical reality. The physical body is not who we are; it is merely the vehicle we "drive" while we are in embodiment on Earth. We are responsible for how we treat our body and, just like our car, the better we take care of it, the better it will serve us.

The lower human ego has tricked us into using our physical body as a status symbol the same way we use cars as a status symbol. If we drive a Rolls Royce, we are perceived as prosperous and successful, but if we drive an old jalopy, we are perceived as poverty-stricken failures. If our physical body fits the currently accepted body type for the times, we feel good about ourself, but if we vary from the acceptable "norm," we feel embarrassed and ashamed of ourself.

As we are embraced in the Love of our Solar Christ Presence, we begin to know and understand that we have created our physical body, and it is providing us with the exact learning experiences we need. To hate our body just delays our progress and perpetuates our misery. What we need to do is learn to Love it and respect it as the beautiful, miraculous organism it is.

Remember, this is a new beginning. You have *no* preconceived ideas about your body. You are neutral and at peace with it. Begin, this moment, by being grateful for the opportunity this intelligent vehicle is providing for you to experience the Earth plane.

> *"Beloved Body Elemental, I thank you for providing me with the opportunity to experience the physical plane so that I may become master of energy, vibration and consciousness, as well as a co-Creator with my Father-Mother God."*

Feel the crystalline pink frequency of gratitude and adoration flowing through the Stargate of your Heart into every cell, organ, function, atom and sub-atomic particle of your physical body. Feel the joy and elation of this vehicle as it begins to, at long last, be revered and respected by you. Maintain this feeling of Love and gratitude for your body throughout the day.

As you bathe your body, feel your hands projecting healing and Love into every single cell. As you rub your hands over your body with soap and water, caress *every* part of your body with tenderness and Love. As you do this, in the embrace of your Solar Christ Presence, you will realize that every inch of your body is beautiful, sensual, receptive and responsive to your

Love. Revel in the sensations of your body as it responds to your Loving, healing caress, and get to know this vehicle as it begins to come alive again and as you allow it to feel and express itself without guilt or shame.

Your body is sensitive and sensual for a reason. The pleasurable feelings you experience when your body is Loved and caressed allow you to feel nurtured, and it encourages you to open the Stargate of your Heart. The beautiful sensations that flow through your body when it is Lovingly touched and caressed trigger chemical changes in the body that enable you to receive and assimilate greater quantities of life force. This increased life force rejuvenates the body and keeps it vibrant and young. It accelerates healing and eliminates the degenerative diseases of aging, which are created by closing down the Heart Center and blocking the flow of life force. The added life force also heals the grief and pain of lost Love, rejection, abandonment, loneliness and despair. It lifts one out of depression and into a sense of well-being and inner peace.

Certain areas of the body are more sensual and erotic than others. By allowing yourself to experience the pleasurable sensations and warm, nurturing feelings of these areas through your healing, Loving touch, you will open the Stargate of your Heart further, and you will feel the greater glow of God's Love filling your Being.

Opening up your feeling nature through the physical sensations of gentle, Loving touch creates within your body a sense of trust, security and safety. As you Love your body and increase the flow of God's Love in, through and around you, you begin to truly **know** that God is the *source* of your Love, constantly filling you up with the Holy Essence of Divine Love. This inner knowing will enable you to understand that as long as you are open and receptive to this connection with God's Love and the Love of your body, no one outside of you can take Love away from you.

Because of the taboos that have been inflicted upon us, often the thought of touching our body in a pleasurable way seems shocking, but you must recognize that that belief is coming from the old patterns of self-deprivation, flagellation and denial. That is no longer who you are. You are now embraced in the Love of your Solar Christ Presence, and through this Divine Consciousness, you will learn to Love and revere every aspect of your Being—etheric, mental, emotional and **physical.**

We have often allowed ourself to feel Love emotionally, but sex is the way we feel and experience Love physically. When you begin to allow your body to awaken to physical sensations with the healing, Loving caress of your own touch, you will feel safe and trusting. At first you may feel uncomfortable and awkward, but that is just because of the old, erroneous taboos. When you begin this process of awakening the wonderful Loving sensations of your body, in the privacy of your own space, consider the activity a sacred and Holy expression of Love between your physical body and your Solar Christ Presence. In truth, there is no way you can fully open your Heart in trust and Love to another person's touch until you first experience the honest and true feeling of Love emotionally and **physically** for yourself and your body. You will find that this process of sensually feeling, caressing, Loving and healing your body through your own tender touch will greatly heighten your ability to safely experience the pleasure of someone else's touch.

When we begin to look at this process through the eyes of reason and common sense, we can logically ask, "Why would it be okay to touch and massage certain areas of our body such as our hands, face, arms, legs and back, but not okay to touch and massage other areas of our body just because they are more sensual and give us greater pleasure?" If we just think about that, we will see that we have obviously been trying to punish and deprive ourself because we perceive our sexuality to be "bad." Now, we know sex is not only not bad, but it is a very important way through which we experience Love physically. Positive sexual experiences enable us to raise and revitalize our body, and they create an atmosphere of trust that empowers us and encourages us to open the Stargate of our Heart without fear.

In addition to Loving our body through nurturing touch, we need to Love it by giving it all of the other physical nourishment it needs as well: healthy, living food; pure water; Sunshine; fresh air and exercise. When we consume anything, we should do so as a sacred repast. Bless all you consume, and send forth your gratitude to the Elemental Kingdom for providing the gift of sustenance.

You will find that as you begin to Love your body, you will want to take care of it in all the necessary ways, just as we take good care of anything else we Love. Through this Love, your body will begin to positively respond, and in an atmosphere of being Loved, instead of loathed, it will be much more able to heal itself and maintain a frequency of vibrant health, radiant beauty and eternal youth.

BEING INTIMATE WITH SOMEONE ELSE

After you truly experience deep Love for your physical body and yourself, you are then ready to allow an intimate relationship into your life. This can mean transforming an intimate relationship that you are already involved in, or it can mean creating a new, intimate relationship. You have to be very careful at this point because this is often when one becomes frightened and tries to close down the Heart Center again. I encourage you to pay very close attention to your feelings, and give yourself as much time as you need to complete the healing process of learning to Love yourself first. Don't force yourself into a sexual relationship with another person too soon. This doesn't give you permission to avoid ever having to get involved with another person though; that would just be more of the same old obsolete pattern of resistance and denial. This is giving you permission to become secure in your new experience of Loving yourself and your body and learning to trust yourself and your sexuality *before* you get involved with someone else. In other sections of this book, I have discussed how to revitalize existing relationships and how to create new relationships, so I won't repeat the process here.

I will assume that you have magnetized into your life a wonderful, nurturing, caring person with whom you want to Lovingly share your sexuality. The person you choose for this very sacred sharing is, of course, your choice. No one outside of you has the right to make that decision for you. No one knows what your life path involves or what learning experiences you have agreed to go through. It is actually rather humorous to observe that some people have given themselves permission to decide who someone else should or should not have sex with. If both people are adults and the decision to be intimately involved with each other is a mutually Loving and positive agreement, then that is all that matters. It is nobody else's business. For us to have the audacity to tell another human being who they can or cannot share this intimate Loving communion with reflects not only the epitome of our arrogance, but the epitome of our ignorance. We need to focus on our own relationships, and we must allow everyone else to do the same.

Once you have, through the open Stargate of your Heart, chosen someone you would like to open up to sexually, in trust and Love, then there are a few helpful thoughts that will allow you to be sure your relationship continues its forward progress based in integrity. Most importantly, you must remember that sexuality is intended to be an expression of Love, a deep, intimate sharing, a sacred communion. This means that it is very important for you and your partner to continually be aware of each other throughout your sexual interaction. You must communicate your needs and your feelings to each other, and express your enjoyment and pleasure. Whatever the two of you choose to experience is your business, as long as you both are in agreement and are interacting with Love, respect and reverence for your physical bodies and each other.

Just as you had to take time to learn to become comfortable while Loving and caressing your own body, you need to be patient and tolerant with both yourself and your partner as you learn to feel safe and comfortable touching and caressing each other's body. But, I promise you, the rewards will be well worth the effort.

Through an open, mutual, Loving, sexual sharing, you will be able to reach into Octaves of Ecstasy that will thrill your Heart and fill your soul. The experience of orgasm has been very distorted in our human minds, but its original Divine Intent was to lift each of us up in frequency and vibration into the higher Realms of Bliss and Joy. This experience was designed to revitalize and expand the Stargate of the Heart in a way that would sustain it as an ever-expanding portal of Divine Love. The experience of orgasm allows you and your partner to reach in consciousness, as one unified force, into higher and higher Octaves of Wonder and Awe.

When you are connecting at a Heart level with a Loving *monogamous* partner, you will grow in leaps and bounds in your ability to express and receive Love and sexual intimacy. You will form a unified chalice through which the healing, nurturing Love of God will continually pour.

Monogamy is a very important part of our success in experiencing the highest level of sexual intimacy. Monogamy means sexually interacting with one person. This doesn't necessarily mean the same person forever, but it means not trying to juggle more than one sexual relationship at a time. When a person gets involved in more than one relationship at a time, s/he is not honoring either partner or him/herself. This destroys a person's integrity, and they become dishonest and deceitful. This self-betrayal causes one to close the Heart Center and hide from who they really are. Their very life becomes a lie, which results in all manner of stress, anxiety, guilt and low self-esteem. This deceit begins to reflect in every facet of their existence, and they experience pain and suffering in all areas, including finances, jobs, health and relationships. It is *never* worth the price we pay when we create a dual life of deception. The ramifications are monumental, and the healing process is excruciating.

Another very important factor in monogamy is that you are an electromagnetic Being, and when you sexually interact with another person, you bond your electromagnetic frequency with your partner. When your frequency is attuned to your partner through Love and reverence, you interact together to lift each other into the Realms of Ecstasy. Two Loving, attuned people can have absolutely profound sexual experiences through the open Stargate of the Heart. If, however, a person is having more than one sexual partner, the electromagnetic bonding becomes fragmented and actually short-circuits the Heart connection. This, combined with the absence of integrity and honesty, results in all kinds of negative backlash within the physical body, and it adds to the emotional chaos in one's feelings as well.

When you are interacting in an open, Loving, monogamous relationship, you can allow yourself to soar into the heights of happiness and joy. You can also reach your highest level of integrity, honesty, loyalty and trustworthiness. This builds your self-confidence and your sense of self-worth, and it enhances your ability to expand the Stargate of your Heart, which lifts you ever higher.

Sexuality is about honoring and Loving yourself, your body, your partner and your partner's body. It is about self-discovery in relationship to your body and your partner. You are raising up in vibration daily and hourly, so when you join bodies with someone else, even in a hug, you exchange frequencies. When you share a sexual experience, there are hormonal releases that occur in both your body and the body of your partner. The hormones awaken certain energies inside the atomic cellular structures of your body, and there is a transfer of your vibrations into your partner and vice versa. For this reason, it is extremely important that you be discriminating with whom you chose to share sexual intimacy. Casual sex is far more detrimental than just the possibility of disease. When you have a sexual experience with someone, you are taking on part of who they are. It is critical that the person you choose to have sex with is in alignment and attuned to you through the open Stargate of your Heart. The only way you will really know this is by getting to know the person very well and communicating with that person with a Loving, open Heart.

As a Loving, sexual relationship develops between two people who are attuned through the open Stargate of the Heart, greater heights of orgasmic experiences can be received. This occurs as the vibration of the physical body is increased to withstand higher frequencies of ecstasy. The nervous system is actually enhanced, and the result is the healing and realignment of the physical body. This process will open us up to higher Octaves of Illumined Truth, and we will experience a whole new dimension of who we are. We will evolve and grow into greater physical expressions of our Solar Christ Presence, and we will more effectively be *God in Action* on Earth.

The expanded awareness we are now receiving about our sexuality will apply to every individual in a different way, according to where each one is in their Earthly sojourn and what their particular Divine Plan entails. Some people are in their latter years and feel the sexual part of their life is complete. Even if one is not interacting sexually with a partner, it is still important for all of us to heal our past negative sexual experiences from this or other lifetimes, and it is important that we learn to Love and revere our body.

Sometimes a person has chosen to experience this physical plane without a partner, and that is perfectly all right, too. You just need to be sure that that is really your Divine Plan and not just a cop-out, so you won't have to risk opening up your Heart. If it is truly your Divine Plan to be without a partner, you will feel an inner peace about it; you won't feel lonely or deprived, and you will be able to open the Stargate of your Heart *fully* without a partner. Again, being without a partner doesn't mean that you ignore your body. You still need to learn to experience the Love of your physical body.

Sometimes people feel they have been forced into celibacy due to a problem with bodily function caused by impotence or spinal injury. If that is the case, it certainly doesn't mean you can't have a Loving, intimate relationship with your partner; it just means you need to be more creative. Remember, *sex is an intimate, Loving communion, through which we experience the heightened ecstasy of Love as we reach out through the Divine portal of the Stargate of the Heart to our partner, connecting Heart, mind and body.* This can be accomplished in a *multitude* of ways. Our means of expressing our sexuality is limited only by the limits of our imagination.

It is time for us to be *liberated* from our distorted belief systems of the past. It is time for us to soar to the heights of bliss, wonder, ecstasy and awe, which are now infinitely available to us through the open Stargate of our Heart.

AFFIRMATION

"I Am" Divine Love pulsating through the open Stargate of my Heart, expanding out to encompass every atom, molecule and cell of my body, raising this vehicle into Limitless Physical Perfection.

"I Am" my Solar Christ Presence liberating my sexuality into the perfection of its original Divine Intent.

So Be It. Beloved "I Am".

CHAPTER
NINE

CREATING NEW RELATIONSHIPS

Wonderful relationships often seem to be an illusive dream. They are something we long for, but don't really believe we are capable of obtaining. Our observation of the "real world" confirms our fears. We see co-dependent, abusive, dysfunctional relationships everywhere. Reports by the media affirm this plight. We are constantly hearing and reading about the lack of available, positive men and women. We read humorous but woeful statistics such as, "A woman over 40 has a better chance of being attacked by a terrorist than she does of finding a meaningful relationship." From the single women I counsel, I believe most of them really believe that. The interesting thing to remember about all of this is that, "Energy follows thought," and what we believe, we bring into form. Most of the people I counsel who are having a hard time manifesting positive relationships really believe their efforts are futile. They believe that they are lacking in some area that would prevent the person they would be attracted to from being attracted to them. I even counseled a man who consistently broke up with every woman who ever Loved him because he said he didn't have any respect for a woman who would Love a loser like himself. Now, that's pretty bad! But, if you are having problems magnetizing wonderful, available relationships into your life, you are probably sending out subtle thoughtforms that are very similar to his. You may intellectually want and desire a wonderful relationship, but in your Heart you may not really believe you are Lovable enough to deserve one. The subtle, sometimes subliminal, attitudes you have about yourself and your worthiness or unworthiness, are usually the greatest blocks in creating positive relationships.

Since people treat us and perceive us the way we feel about ourself, we are continually drawing people to us who will confirm our belief systems. That is why it is said that our relationships are mirror reflections of what is going on within us.

This doesn't necessarily mean we are just like the person, but it means that if the person we are with is abusive or disrespectful, or does not honor us or Love us in a deep nurturing way, then *we also do not Love, honor or respect ourself.* This is not a theory. This is the scientific law of action and reaction and like attracts like. We may be in denial about how we feel about ourself, and we may be affirming, " 'I Am' Lovable, and I deserve Loving relationships," but if we are not manifesting them in our life, then there is some underlying block that is preventing them from happening. Unless we are willing to release our low self-esteem and our erroneous beliefs of unworthiness, then we will perpetually be on the roller coaster of dysfunctional relationships.

Now, the good news! Everything has changed with the opening of the Stargate of the Heart. We no longer have to play out the excruciating treadmill of the "Wheel of Karma" regarding our relationships. For aeons of time, our Heart Center was closed, and the magnetic force that attracted our relationships into our life was the energy field around us that was filled with every thought, word, action or feeling we had about ourself. This energy field was perceived as reality regardless of how distorted or inaccurate our beliefs were. With the opening of the Stargate of the Heart, we have accessed a multi-dimensional frequency of ourself that transcends the illusion of the fallen human ego. We have accessed the Feeling Nature of God, the Feminine Polarity of God, the Divine Mother. There is not another aspect of God that will more effectively lift us into the wisdom and knowledge of our true reality. There is not another facet of Divinity that will reveal to us more clearly the glory and wonder of who we really are. Once this Divine Truth begins to resonate in our Heart, never again will we feel unworthy of having Loving, wonderful relationships, and never again will we need to experience the pain of abandonment, rejection, abuse, loneliness and every other mutation that was created when we closed our Heart Center to the Love of God.

The opening of the Stargate of the Heart has created a portal through which the Love of our Mother God can continually flow into, through and around every atomic and sub-atomic particle of our Being, filling every electron of our physical, etheric, mental and emotional bodies with the Divine Love of God. If you will focus on this Divine activity of Light, every frequency of low self-esteem, unworthiness, self-loathing, doubt, fear, anxiety, etc., will be Transmuted into the reality of your God Self. When you are resonating with the Divine Love of our Mother God, through every fiber of your Being, it is impossible to magnetize abusive relationships into your life. When you are filled with the Divine Love of our Mother God, the forcefield around you will be magnetizing relationships into your sphere of influence that are reverberating with Divine Love as well.

In the embrace of the Love of our Mother God, you will not be willing to remain in situations that do not reflect your value and your worth as a Child of God. You will experience a reverence and Love for yourself that will not tolerate abuse of any kind.

Now that the Stargate of the Heart is open, we do not have to just sit around and wait for things to change in our life. We can actively participate in changing our self-image and our relationships. We need to begin by clearing out all of the old, erroneous belief system that reflect any sense of unworthiness. As you know by now, there is nothing more effective in clearing negativity than the Violet Flame of Limitless Transmutation. This Sacred Violet Fire is the perfect balance of the Sapphire Blue Ray of our Father God's Divine Power and the Crystalline Pink Ray of our Mother God's Divine Love. When we invoke It into our misqualified thoughts, words, actions and feelings, there is not one electron of energy that can resist Its Transmuting power. The process of utilizing this Sacred Flame is very simple. It *must* respond to the Divinity of our God Presence according to Cosmic Law, so all we have to do is command It into action through the power of our mighty "I Am" Presence. You can certainly create your own invocation, but it is as easy as saying:

Through the power of the Almighty Presence of God "I Am" blazing in my Heart, I invoke the Violet Flame of Limitless Transmutation from the very Heart of my Father-Mother God to blaze in, through and around every electron of precious life energy I have ever misqualified in any time frame or dimension, both known and unknown, back to my inception. I command the Violet Flame to Transmute the cause, core, effect, record and memory of every thought, word, action or feeling I have ever had that is in any way preventing me from fulfilling my Divine Birthright as a child of God. Through the power of this Sacred Fire, "I Am" lifted into the Realms of Illumined Truth, and I now KNOW the truth of who "I Am". I accept, through all facets of wisdom and understanding, that "I Am" worthy of living the life my Father-Mother God intended for me to live. And I now accept full responsibility for my part in co-Creating a life of Joy, Limitless Abundance, Vibrant Health, Loving Relationships, Fulfilling Career, Eternal Peace, Happiness, Laughter and Success in fulfilling my Divine Plan.

I ask that the Violet Flame of Limitless Transmutation now blazing through every fiber of my Being, be maintained, eternally self-sustained, increased daily and hourly, moment to moment, the maximum that Cosmic Law will allow, until "I Am" wholly Ascended and Free.

I accept that this invocation has been ACCOMPLISHED with full power, for I have made it in God's most holy name, "I Am".

It is done! So be it!

"I Am"

As we repeat this invocation DAILY, it will build in effectiveness and momentum, thus increasing in power until every trace of our distorted perception of low self-esteem is gone. This exercise is the equivalent of removing from our computer the old "floppy disc" with the wrong program on it. It is a *critical* step in creating new, wonderful relationships.

Now, as we are Transmuting the past through the daily use of the Violet Flame of Limitless Transmutation, we can *simultaneously* create our new "program." In order to do this, we need to create a vision of who we really are. This is a thoughtform that actually forms a blueprint that is projected onto the atomic cellular structure of our four lower bodies. Our thoughts and feelings are creative, so all we have to do to accomplish this positive blueprint of who we are is envision it.

To begin this process, sit comfortably in your chair with your spine as straight as possible and your arms and legs uncrossed. (Have a pencil and paper handy to write down your vision.) Now, take some slow, deep breaths. As you breathe *in,* feel yourself reaching in consciousness through the open portal of the Stargate of your Heart into the Octaves of Illumined Truth. There you absorb and assimilate the full-gathered momentum of Divine Love from our Mother God. As you breathe *out,* that Divine Love flows through the open portal of the Stargate of your Heart into every electron of your Being, bathing you in the radiance of our Mother's Love. With every *inbreath,* you reach higher into the Perfection of Divine Love, and with every *outbreath,* you project that Divine Love into your Being and World. Feel and experience the glory of this Love. Know and recognize that this is the feeling nature of God that we mistakenly separated ourself from when we fell from Grace aeons ago. Feel the elation of our Mother God as She once again embraces Her Beloved Child. This is the fulfillment of the allegory of the "prodigal son." We have returned home with contrite Hearts to the arms of our Father-Mother God, and within the embrace of Divine Love and Forgiveness, we are now capable of fulfilling our incomprehensible potential.

The Love of God, which is now flowing through the Stargate of your Heart, prepares the RNA/DNA structures of your genetic codes to receive the new patterns of your perfection. Through the power of your God Presence "I Am", you begin to co-Create with our Father-Mother God the vision of who you really are.

Deep within your Heart Flame ask yourself, "If I could be the most whole, complete, powerful, positive, Loving force of good on the Planet, who would I be?" Now, gently take your pencil and paper and write down the thoughts that come to you. Don't analyze or censure your thoughts at this point, just let them flow through you onto the paper. Don't feel self-conscious or egotistical; just keep reaching higher and higher, daring to dream of your own outlandish magnificence.

I promise you, no matter how glorious your vision is or how limitless it is in its perfection, you will only be scratching the surface of who you really are.

After you have completed your writing, take another piece of paper and make a permanent list of positive affirmations of the vision of the "new you." Word it always in a positive way. Don't worry about whether you actually believe you are expressing all of the concepts now or not. Remember, this is a blueprint, and by focusing on the new patterns and affirming them daily with DEEP FEELING, they will begin to integrate into your behavior patterns. You will not think of anything that you are incapable of becoming. Remember, "WHAT THE MIND CAN CONCEIVE, THE PERSON CAN ACHIEVE."

Don't feel like you are deceiving yourself by affirming things that haven't manifested yet. That is the whole point. *You are creating a new reality.* Again, you must "FAKE IT 'TIL YOU MAKE IT!"

The following is just an example. You may use it as a guide, but it is very important for you to tailor your list to express the perfect YOU.

"I Am"

1. **"I Am"** Filled with the Love of my Father-Mother God.

2. **"I Am"** Happy and experiencing the Joy of God's Limitless Abundance in every facet of my life. "I Am" financially FREE!

3. **"I Am"** Vibrantly Healthy, Radiantly Beautiful (Handsome), Eternally Youthful. "I Am" slim, firm, flawless form.

4. **"I Am"** working in a job that is richly rewarding, both creatively and financially. I look forward to each day with expectancy and enthusiasm.

5. **"I Am"** in a romantic relationship that fills my very Being with Elation and Bliss. My partner is nurturing and supportive; compassionate and tender; an excellent listener and communicator; a dear friend and companion; a passionate, romantic lover; a source of comfort and solace; excitement and fun; humor and laughter; peace and security; Love and happiness. He (She) is financially secure, healthy, physically attractive to me, spiritually compatible with me, growing and eagerly fulfilling his (her) Divine Plan and striving toward his (her) highest potential. We are interested in the same type of commitment, and he (she) is now physically and emotionally available for this relationship. He (She) Loves and reveres me for who "I Am", just the way "I Am" now, and he (she) is also anxious to grow with me into my highest potential. He (She) is secure, confident, devoted and courageous. He (She) is comfortable, allowing me the space to be who "I Am", and he (she) feels good enough about himself (herself) to allow me to soar to the heights of who "I Am".

We integrate easily into each other's worlds. Our families are compatible and a nurturing source of Love and friendship.

We mutually honor, respect and revere each other, and our

Life together is filled with Love, Laughter and abounding Joy.

6.   **"I Am"** an effective, competent, powerful source of good in every facet of my life.

7.   **"I Am"** clearly connected to my God Presence and the Realms of Illumined Truth. I continually listen for Divine Guidance, and I easily and effortlessly respond to every situation that occurs in my life with Divine Discerning Intelligence. My decisions and choices always reflect the highest good for all concerned, and with every breath I take, "I Am" adding to the Light of the world.

8.   **"I Am"** a source of comfort and nurturing for everyone and everything within my sphere of influence.

9.   **"I Am"** surrendering my lower human ego to the full power and authority of my God Presence. Through this activity of Light, "I Am" a consistent transmitter of God's Perfection into the world of form.   "I Am" the open door that no one can shut. "I Am" a cup, a Holy Grail, through which the Light of God will pour to Love all life free, and "I Am" eternally grateful for the honor and privilege of being a Child of God in embodiment on Earth during Her glorious rebirth.

So be it!

Once you have Transmuted your past, distorted low self-esteem and negative self-image and created the positive image of the "new you," which you are affirming everyday, you are ready for the next step, which is actually manifesting your perfect relationship.

To create a wonderful relationship, you must first clearly evaluate what a wonderful relationship would be for you. Spend some time and ask yourself, "What do I want in a relationship?" Most people have all kinds of lists of what they don't want, but fairly sketchy thoughts about what they do want. Since our thoughts are creative, when we only have a fragmented idea of what we want, we keep drawing fragmented relationships into our life. So make a very specific, detailed list. Look around you and pay attention to all of the qualities and characteristics you Love about people. Then, look at the things you don't like and ask yourself, "What do I want instead of that?" Evaluate every facet of the relationship. Number 5 in the preceding "I Am" list will give you an idea of some positive attributes for a relationship; but your list needs to be even more all-encompassing than that.

Begin your list by writing...

"I Am" magnetizing into my life, in Divine Timing, my ideal relationship. He (She) fulfills all of the following qualities and characteristics:

(Then list everything that you can think of that you want in a relationship and always word it in a positive way.)

To energize this process into physical manifestation, you must focus on ALL THREE STEPS *everyday* until your dream relationship comes true.

1. Invoke the Violet Flame of Limitless Transmutation.
2. Affirm the "I Am" vision of the "new you."
3. Affirm the list for your ideal relationship.

Continually work in the eternal moment of NOW. Know that, in Divine Timing, your God Presence will draw the perfect person to you. Give the Universe every opportunity to respond. Get out and meet people. Socialize. Be active. Do things you Love with other people. Have fun. Laugh. Be yourself.

You deserve a wonderful relationship, but remember, a

relationship is only the icing on the cake, NOT the *source* of your Love or Happiness. Once you really accept this truth, then *never again will you allow another person to devastate you to the point of closing down your Heart Center. And never again will you disconnect from the Divine Love of our Father-Mother God.*

This powerful force of Love, which is now flowing through the open Stargate of our Heart, will keep us perpetually in the nurturing embrace of our Mother's Love. As long as we strive to keep our Heart Center open and absorb the magnificence of this Divine Love, we will never again experience the feeling of *not* being Loved. No matter what learning experiences we are going through in our relationships, we will KNOW that the bonds of Love with our Father-Mother God are eternal and all-encompassing. This Divine Knowledge will create a security in us that will transcend all of the past pain of rejection. It will create an inner peace and trust that will enable us to keep our Heart Center open with confidence and safety. And it will allow each of us to be the powerful transmitters of Divine Love we are destined to be. What a glorious opportunity.

Thank you, God!

CHAPTER TEN

REVITALIZING EXISTING RELATIONSHIPS

Because life is so hectic, we often just allow our relationships to exist on "automatic pilot." We know we Love our partner, so we take for granted the probability that s/he also knows we Love him/her. We take for granted the probability that our partner still Loves us, too. We communicate to get the necessary survival things accomplished each day, and we interact in passing as we are on our way to our other daily responsibilities. Our job, the children and things we must do around the house generally create what seems like an all-consuming challenge. We feel we have to get everything done, so if we have any time at all for ourself or a social life, it seems like a miracle. This chaotic lifestyle has taken over the majority of families, and as a result, we are experiencing rampant divorce, abuse, neglect, alcoholism and drug abuse, dysfunctional behavior patterns and the tragic demise of healthy family life. Through this sad scenario, we are cheating ourself out of some of the most fulfilling and rewarding experiences we are capable of having in this third dimensional reality.

Divine Family Life was originally supposed to be part of our learning experience on Earth. The nurturing, Loving, open sharing that is possible in a family situation doesn't exist in the same intensity in any other relationship. I know that most families are not expressing their highest potential (to say the least), but that doesn't change the fact that we truly do have the ability to create a wonderful family life. Like everything else, our family life reflects what we are feeling and believing about ourself. In order to begin improving our family interactions and our relationships with our spouse or partner, once again, we need to get in touch with how we are Loving or not loving ourself.* Depending on how we feel about ourself at any given moment, we can either let things "push our buttons," hurt our feelings and

See Chapter 3 for specifics on Learning to Love Yourself.

make us angry; **or** we can listen with greater clarity, have more patience and understanding, and perceive viable solutions to the problem. As you can see, those responses are diametrically opposed, and the outcome of the situation will be entirely different, depending on where we are coming from mentally and emotionally. One outcome will be constructive and the other will just add to the quagmire of our pain and confusion.

It's hard to believe sometimes that our opinion about ourself could really have such a monumental effect on every single thing that is occurring in our life, BUT IT DOES!!! At any given moment, we are outpicturing who we believe we are. Our opinion of ourself varies depending on what we have been going through in our life. If things have been going well, we often feel confident and good about ourself. If things seem to be going wrong, we usually feel victimized, and we feel like a failure.

Everyday we allow the challenges we are going through to determine how we feel about ourself. First thing in the morning we look at our day, and then we climb on the "roller coaster of emotions" to ride out the rest of the day. If things go well, we feel great; if things go poorly we feel bad—up and down, up and down, over and over again. This emotional roller coaster creates such a drain on our energy level that we feel depleted and exhausted by mid-day. Our efficiency level drops, and by the time we return home to our family, we are like a zombie, barely able to raise our fork to our mouth for dinner, let alone carry on a meaningful conversation. Our Heart Center is closed, and we just want to be left alone. Our level of patience is non-existent, and even the slightest problem seems monumental. Because we are in our own home and we feel safe there, we give ourself permission to vent our frustrations at whomever is within earshot. We often allow the smallest challenge to be the catalyst for us to release our tension and, consequently, we blow our top at the very people we Love the most. Needless to say, this is not only extremely unfair, it is incredibly destructive, and it destroys our family relationships. It is time for us to change these dysfunctional behavior patterns and, fortunately, we have the ability to do it. We just need to create a new attitude and a new belief system about what is real and true.

Amazingly, the previous scenario is so common that it seems as though we all must be functioning under the influence of some form of mass hypnosis and, in a way, we are. Remember, all life is interrelated, and if enough people are creating thoughtforms of a particular belief system, it forms a forcefield of mass consciousness that influences everyone who is within its embrace. If we will just review some of the beliefs people have about everyday life, we will clearly see how we are being adversely influenced by the mass thoughtforms of others. The majority of people have a belief system that supports the illusion that...

There is not enough time in the day to get everything done.

Money is very hard to come by and will always be a difficult struggle.

Work is stressful, exhausting, unfulfilling and boring.

There are always going to be major problems in every relationship.

I don't have time to take care of me. I don't have time to prepare healthy meals or exercise, etc.

I don't have time for a social life.

Aging and the degeneration of the physical body is an inevitable part of life.

Parents and teenagers never understand each other.

Men and women never understand each other.

All of the good men are taken. All of the good women are taken.

Communication is a very difficult part of any relationship.

Men aren't able to express emotions.

Men are usually not emotionally available.

Women are too sensitive and too emotional.

Men are only interested in sex.

Women don't feel as intensely about sex as men do.

I am a victim of my childhood.

I am not smart enough.

I am not pretty/handsome enough.

I am not healthy enough.

I am not wealthy enough.

I am not _____ enough.
                (Fill in the blank)

One person can't possibly make a difference in the overall scheme of things.

All governments are corrupt.

Crime is inevitable.

The streets aren't safe.

Pollution is going to destroy the Earth.

The condition of the Planet appears to be tragically hopeless.

Etc., etc., etc.

Now, we can read this list of beliefs and say, "Well, of course people believe these things, because they *are* true. Just look around." I realize from outer appearances they certainly do seem true, but the problem is we are forgetting just how life in the physical plane works. We are looking at life and saying, "That is reality," when in truth, in order for something to manifest in the physical plane, IT MUST *FIRST* BE HELD IN THE CONSCIOUSNESS OF SOMEONE ABIDING IN THAT DIMENSION. In other words, in order for us to experience not having enough time to get everything done, we must FIRST *believe* we don't have enough time to get everything done. In order for us to be struggling with money, we must FIRST *believe* money is hard to come by. In order for us to be in dysfunctional relationships, we must FIRST *believe* that we are unworthy of loving, positive relationships, or else we must believe that the "right" person doesn't exist for us.

These belief systems are often very subtle, and they are formed by our distorted perception. We simply look at life and say, *"That is what's true,"* instead of looking at life and saying, ***"That only* appears *to be true because I'm accepting it as truth. If I want to change my reality, I merely need to change my* belief *in what I accept as truth."***

For instance, if we begin to actually create a new belief system and energize it with our thoughts and feelings, our physical reality will gradually change to reflect our new belief system.

I know that in analytical psychology, we can take each and every situation that is out of order in our life and dissect it. We can evaluate it and try to determine what the cause is and how the problem developed, etc. But, this process can take a whole lifetime with very little progress being made in the end.

We are in a very unique time on Earth and the whole paradigm of reality is shifting. Due to the incredible acceleration we have experienced in vibration and consciousness over recent years, we are in a whole new place. Things don't work the way they used to, and our ability to change things is becoming much, much easier. If that isn't occurring in your life, then it is probably because you still *believe* change has to be a slow and difficult process. The exciting thing about this paradigm shift is that it is affecting the physical experience on Earth, whether we fully understand it or not. We don't need to intellectually grasp every facet of this transformation in order to implement it effectively into our Earthly experience. We may try to make it mind boggling and complicated, but it is really very simple. It is a slight adjustment in our awareness.

Rather than trying to dissect everything that is wrong in our life and rehash it to death, all we have to do is *let it go.* Now, I know that seems over-simplified, but it is really *just that easy.* There are a multitude of modalities and various techniques to help us heal the past and make peace with our inner child, etc. Most of them are effective to a degree, but they still involve a very long, arduous process. Some people feel they *need* to go through the process so that they will understand everything about the experience in order to be able to let it go. If they *believe* that, then they will create it. But what I am really striving to impress on you now is that *we no longer need to do that.* We are creating our own reality on Earth, and if we *accept* the *truth* that we can let go of the past negative experience, just like taking the old floppy disc with the wrong program on it out of the computer and inserting a new disc with the correct program on it, then we can make it our reality, and it will be just that simple.

We are creatures of habit, and because we are so used to living in limitation and feeling victimized by life, letting go of the past seems as though it is easier said than done. But, the important thing for us to keep reiterating to ourself is that it is *very possible,* and with our consistent efforts, we're going to be victorious.

The process of letting go means just that. It does not mean stuffing or being in denial or suppressing our feelings. And it doesn't mean ignoring the lesson or pretending like the experience didn't happen, either. Letting go is accomplished as we lift up in consciousness and see the greater picture. *We are all going through the learning experiences that we need for our growth, and we are all going through the experiences that, at some level, we have agreed to go through.* When we understand that, it moves us out of the poor me, victim role and helps us to look at the experience as an opportunity to learn and grow. Knowing that we have gone through the experiences that we agreed at higher levels to go through, and knowing that the people, places, conditions and things involved in the experiences were just the instruments, the Universe used to bring those growth opportunities to us, then it removes the feeling of injustice, anger and criticism toward the situation and the people involved. We realize if it wasn't that particular person, place, condition or thing the Universe would just find another person, place, condition or thing to bring the same learning experience to us because the experience contains a lesson we *must* learn for our continual growth and progress, or we wouldn't be going through it in the first place.

Okay, so to begin creating our new reality, we need to change the way we perceive our life. Knowing that our thoughts and feelings are creative, we can create a paradigm shift in our own consciousness away from limitation and into limitless freedom. Energy follows thought, and we have the ability to direct the Light of God into a situation to change it. This process may seem too simple, but it absolutely works. I'm going to use the example of rejuvenating an existing relationship, but you will get the idea, and then you can tailor this process to change any existing challenge in your life.

I will begin with the assumption that you have been working with the tools, and you have learned to Love and respect yourself. As a result of this *very necessary first step*, you are now recognizing that you are truly worthy and deserving of a healthy, Loving relationship. (Remember, this process can be translated into any situation, so through Loving yourself you will also realize you are worthy and deserving of prosperity, youth, health, a fulfilling job, peace, happiness, joy, harmonious family life, success in all your ventures, a wonderful sense of purpose, etc.)

To begin the process of letting go, simply visualize yourself walking through two massive Golden Doors. See all of the "old baggage" associated with the relationship you are interested in rejuvenating being left behind. See and know that the negativity in the relationship existed in order to reflect back to you certain lessons you needed to learn about yourself. People see us and treat us the way we feel about ourself, so our relationships are mirrors reflecting back to us how we feel about ourself and what we need to learn. This is true even if we don't recognize it on a conscious level.

Visualize the baggage being left behind in a way that makes it very tangible and real to you, not just abstract. Some people visualize actual pieces of luggage with labels on them such as: ANGER, FEAR, REJECTION, POOR COMMUNICATION, DISRESPECT, LACK OF LOVE, INFIDELITY, DECEP-TION, HURT, POVERTY, BOREDOM, SUBSTANCE ABUSE, PHYSICAL ABUSE, INDIFFERENCE, LACK OF INTEREST, DISAPPOINTMENT, LACK OF AFFECTION, LACK OF COMMITMENT, CO-DEPENDENCY, POOR SEX LIFE, etc. After you clearly see all of the "old baggage," turn and walk through the Golden Doors.

As you walk away from the baggage and pass through the Golden Doors, the doors close behind you. At that point you invoke the full-gathered momentum of the Violet Flame of Limitless Transmutation:

Through the power of God blazing in my Heart, I invoke

the most intensified activity of the Violet Flame of Limitless Transmutation "I Am" capable of withstanding. Blessed Flame, blaze continually in, through and around every electron of precious life energy that is in any way, shape or form responsible for creating the negative experiences I have left behind the Golden Doors. Transmute the cause, core, effect, record and memory of those experiences and situations back into God's Perfection.

Feel and *know* that the Violet Flame is performing Its Divine Alchemy daily and hourly, building in intensity until every electron of the "old baggage" is Transmuted into Light.

JUST LET IT GO!!!

Now, look before you, and through the eyes of Divine Discerning Intelligence, see the vision of your relationship and your life as you *want* them to be. This is a little bit tricky because sometimes we are in a relationship with someone who was never intended by our God Presence to be our lifetime partner, but rather just a participant in a learning experience to reveal to us how we are Loving or, more accurately, not Loving ourself. So, I want you to please read the following words over very carefully. Sometimes we think we are so in Love with a person that we want to make the relationship work, no matter what. We refuse to admit what is wrong, and we put our blinders on, so that we can comfortably live in denial. We may think that we are avoiding a lot of pain by doing that, but in reality, we are cheating ourself out of one of the most wonderful experiences we can have in this dimension, and that is the genuine, fulfilling Love of a healthy relationship.

Don't panic! I promise you if you are not with your lifetime partner, you will not have to move out of the relationship until it is right for you to do so, and when it is right, you will know it and feel positive about your decision. In the meantime, since you don't know for sure if you are with your lifetime partner or not, just assume that s/he is, and work as though you can transform the relationship into what you want it to be. *But, you must then give your God Presence and the Universe the space to adjust your course by affirming daily...*

"I Am" open and receptive to transforming my existing relationship into its perfect expression according to my DIVINE PLAN. If____(name)____is my lifetime partner, "I Am" grateful. If s/he is not, then "I Am" open and receptive to allowing my lifetime partner into my life, according to the highest good for all concerned. "I Am" creating the space to allow the transition, if it is necessary, to take place in an atmosphere of comfort, Love and inner peace for all involved."

Once you have made your commitment to your Divine Plan and the highest good for all concerned, you have given your "I Am" Presence permission to intervene in the most positive way. Now you are free to focus on revitalizing your relationship without the *fear* that you might force it to continue, even though it may not be for your highest good. You can truly say to yourself, " 'I Am' going to give this relationship my very best shot. I have everything to gain and nothing to lose. If it is in alignment with my Divine Plan, it will be transformed. If it is not, it won't be, but something better will manifest for both of us as a result of my efforts."

For a word of encouragement, I'd like to say that in my experience as a counselor, I believe that, by far, the majority of relationships *can* be transformed into wonderful, Loving expressions of friendship, romance, passion, joy and happiness. When you really work with this process and truly change the way you feel about yourself, the people in your sphere of influence automatically change the way they feel about you, too, and they interact and respond to you differently. This seems like an amazing phenomenon, but it simply confirms the fact that we really do create our own reality.

Revitalizing an existing relationship can be tons of fun. It actually creates an opportunity to fall in Love all over again, and it makes everything new and exciting.

First of all, you need to think back and remember why you fell in Love with your partner in the first place. In great detail, recall what you Loved about him/her.

How did you express your Love for each other?
What fun, Loving things did you do together?
How did you communicate your feelings?
How did you accept and revel in your partner's Love for you?
What tender, nurturing things did you do for each other to demonstrate your Love?
In what ways were you affectionate?
In what ways were you romantic?

Remember your feelings of anticipation at the prospect of talking to each other on the phone or seeing each other or being with each other. Remember the butterflies in your stomach when you touched; the elation when you kissed; the ecstasy when you made Love. All of these experiences were very real to you, and they were perpetuated by your thoughts and feelings. You consciously chose to Love this person, and by focusing your attention on the wonderful things you Loved about him/her, you amplified those qualities in your mind and Heart.

Regardless of what your relationship may have deteriorated into, those qualities that you fell in Love with are still there. And, by focusing your attention on them, you can awaken them in your Loved one and bring them to the surface again. So many times we fall into the very bad habit of just focusing on what is Consequently, through the power of our attention, we amplify the very things we don't want to exist in our relationship. We allow the painful experiences to consume us and, unfortunately, the good things get buried in the confusion. It is critical in the process of revitalizing your existing relationship that you *CONSTANTLY* remember..."WHERE MY ATTENTION IS, THERE 'I AM'! WHAT I PUT MY THOUGHTS AND FEELINGS INTO, I BRING INTO FORM."

Pay very close attention to what you are thinking and feeling about your relationship and your partner, and continually ask yourself, "IS THIS WHAT I WANT TO BE AMPLIFYING IN MY RELATIONSHIP?" If it is *not*, then say to yourself, "WHAT DO I WANT INSTEAD OF THIS?," and put your attention on what you *want,* instead of what you *don't want.*

Make a *long* list of all of the things you ever Loved about your partner. Go over the list *daily.* In your mind's eye, see your partner expressing all of those wonderful qualities. Affirm that s/he is once again emulating all of the Loving potential s/he is capable of expressing. See yourself demonstrating all of the Loving potential you are capable of expressing with your partner as well. See yourselves interacting in the most Loving, positive, mutually respectful way you can envision.

Fantasize about being with each other in the most romantic, nurturing, Loving ways, and then *act out your fantasies.* You will be amazed at how this simple exercise changes your feelings toward your partner. When you start looking at this person through the eyes of Love and acceptance, it totally changes your perspective of him/her. The things that were bothering you before are now balanced with a renewed awareness of the things you Love about the person as well. This new outlook puts the problems in perspective, and they become less looming and all-pervading. Your level of patience and tolerance is greatly increased as well as your willingness to cooperate and compromise. When you are interacting with your partner with an open, Loving Heart, you will see viable solutions to problems that the old emotions of resentment and anger blocked.

Loving relationships don't just happen. Maybe the initial attraction just happens, but the long-term relationship needs Loving, nurturing cultivation. It can never be taken for granted and expected to flourish. Love takes your conscious effort, your time and your energy.

Once you have renewed the thoughts and feelings of what you want your relationship to be, you need to take the steps necessary to manifest it. Make your relationship your **number one priority**. Affirm to yourself, *"I have all the time and space I need to accomplish what I must do today **including** devoting quality time to my relationship."*

To begin healing the pain of the past, you need to take the risk of opening up to your partner and reaching out to him/her, even in the face of adversity. I know this feels a little bit scary, but someone has to break the pattern of closing down and withdrawing. Make up your mind that this is a *process,* and as you persist in reaching out to your partner with Love and acceptance, you will eventually tear down even the densest wall. Decide that you are going to keep flooding your partner with Loving thoughts, feelings and actions even if s/he doesn't initially respond. In other words, be willing to Love him/her unconditionally, expecting nothing in return, knowing that your Love will always be expanded and returned to you by our Father-Mother God.

We have become so adept at numbing ourself to pain that we aren't about to just blatantly trust someone again. We aren't willing to make ourself vulnerable by opening up too quickly even when we feel the vibration of genuine Love. So, you must be patient and honest with your Loved one and, above all, consistent and trustworthy.

Use the Violet Flame to Transmute all of the negativity that ever passed between the two of you, and Transmute any fear, anxiety or doubt that may be blocking either of you from experiencing your deep Heart feelings.

Now, each and everyday, do what you need to do to fill your Heart with joy and Love:

1. Take time *every single day* to open your Hearts, and talk to each other.

2. Tell your partner how much you Love him/her.

3. Communicate specifically about the special things you Love about your partner.

4. Be demonstrative in your affection.

5. Do the tender, Loving, caring things that show your Love without words.

6. Nurture and pamper yourself and your partner.

7. Create wonderful, romantic adventures.

8. Plan to have special romantic, sexy interludes a few times every week.

9. Look forward to the fun time you are going to spend together *everyday*.

10. Schedule quality time for talking, listening, being, supporting and Loving.

11. Be creative and adventurous. Experiment with new ideas and activities.

12. Have fun! Have fun! Have fun!

Buoyant joyous energy is the most rejuvenating, revitalizing frequency of vibration we can experience.

We are here to Love life free *AND* have a ball in the process.   Just Do It !!!
XXX OOO

CHAPTER
ELEVEN

BECOMING A POWERFUL FORCE
OF LOVE ON EARTH

The Power of Our Attention

The Solar Christ Presence has returned to Earth!

Okay, so what does that mean, and what do we do now?

What it means is that, at long last, we have raised up in energy, vibration and consciousness effectively enough to transcend the mud puddle of human miscreation we have been buried in. It means the density of the psychic-astral plane, the "veil of maya" surrounding the Earth, has been Transmuted enough to allow the radiance of our Solar Christ Presence to shine on Earth once again. It means our Ascension into the Octaves of Harmony and Balance is fast becoming a physical, tangible reality. And it means the Transfiguration of this Sweet Planet into Her Divine Heritage of Heaven on Earth IS ASSURED.

What we do now is the critical factor.

What we do now will determine how quickly our Solar Christ Presence will regain full authority of our four lower bodies. What we do now will determine how peacefully and gently the Earth's Transfiguration from discord into harmony will occur. What we do now will greatly affect how soon our limited physical reality will be transformed into Limitless Physical Perfection. And, what we do now will deeply affect whether we move through these unprecedented Earth changes filled with hope, joy and expectancy or fear, pain and anxiety. The **choice is up to us.**

In order for us to fully understand the significance of this opportunity, I would like to reiterate a basic truth.

WHERE YOUR ATTENTION IS, THERE YOU ARE.
WHAT YOU PUT YOUR ATTENTION
AND ENERGY INTO,
YOU BRING INTO FORM!

The Law of Attraction is actually a Creative Force. It is the Light from the Universal Source of All Life that flows through us constantly. As this Light flows through us, *It picks up the particular vibrations of our consciousness* and expresses those vibrations in visible form, experience and circumstance. Our consciousness is always a sum total of our beliefs, thoughts, words, actions and feelings.

We are truly co-Creators with our Father-Mother God. In fact, our whole purpose and reason for being on Earth is to learn how to use our creative faculties of thought and feeling, so that we can become masters of energy, vibration and consciousness on the physical plane and develop the ability to co-Create Heaven on Earth, thus fulfilling the Divine Intent of "As above, so below."

Needless to say, we lost our way, and we have forgotten why we are here. The result of that confusion has created all of the maladies we are now experiencing on Earth. We became submerged in the chaos and confusion, and we lost the awareness of the Law of Attraction. We started focusing on all of the things that were wrong in our life: poverty, disease, loneliness, corruption, crime, devasting weather conditions, destructive Earth changes, etc.

Unfortunately, we haven't realized that by focusing on these negative situations, we are actually perpetuating them. The more our mass consciousness focuses on human afflictions and suffering, the more energy we give to these gross mutations. Through the Law of Attraction, our attention is amplifying the painful conditions on Earth and, sadly, sustaining them. This is a very serious problem at the moment, and it is a destructive pattern that must be reversed immediately if we are to move through the Earth's rebirth harmoniously and unscathed.

So, once again, we are being asked to lift up in consciousness into the Realms of Illumined Truth where, through our own Enlightenment, we will clearly perceive the need of the hour.

We are in a unique time when many people are awakening to the fact that we are multi-dimensional Beings. We function on many levels of consciousness and in many dimensions simultaneously, including the Realms of Perfection, Timelessness and Illumined Truth. We are currently tapping into many different levels of information. Some of the information is coming from the lower psychic-astral realm of deception that is specifically committed to confusing us and blocking us from progressing forward into the Light. Some information is coming from discarnate souls who are trying to help but are only able to give us their own opinion of what is going on, so they aren't any more accurate than someone in the limited physical plane would be. Some of the information is coming from the so-called E.T.s, which are entities from other Star Systems who are supposedly trying to help and guide us. Some information is coming from Illumined Beings in the Realms of Truth Who actually can perceive, with clarity, the need of the hour. These Beings are referred to as the Spiritual Hierarchy. And some information is coming from our own God Presence "I Am", Who is One with the All-Encompassing Presence of God.

Now, in addition to these inter-dimensional sources, we are constantly bombarded with information from the various world religions, governments, news media, scientists, researchers, theorists, visionaries, teachers, employers, friends and family members. It's no wonder that we often walk around feeling like blithering idiots with our brain circuits blown and our minds like mush.

The humorous thing is that in the midst of all of this information, misinformation and disinformation, we are supposed to develop the Divine Discerning Intelligence to filter out everything but the ILLUMINED TRUTH THAT WILL SET

US FREE. Well, lots of luck.

The problem is that the forces of imbalance lie to us when we mistakenly connect with them, and they try to block our Ascension into the Light. After all, this is the force of deception, and they know we are not stupid. They don't say, "I am the sinister force, and I have come to ruin your life." They say, "I'm God, follow me." They always give us enough truth (according to our belief system) to make us believe we have connected with a knowledgeable source of information. Then, once we are open and trusting, they gently, and sometimes not so gently, lead us "down the garden path," throwing in tidbits of information that will perpetuate Humanity's suffering instead of Transmuting it into harmony and balance.

We really have a job on our hands. I know that trying to develop *Divine Discerning Intelligence* sometimes seems like an act in futility, but it is the most important skill we can develop at this time. After all, when we really grasp the magnitude of the Universal Law of Attraction, all we have to do is monitor our thoughts, words, actions and feelings for a single day to realize that practically every minute we are focusing on some negative aspect of our life that we don't want to amplify. Consistently, we are energizing with our thoughts and feelings: relationship problems, financial problems, job problems, family problems, world problems, failure consciousness, low self-esteem and every other conceivable thing we choose to worry about. We may, spasmodically, throw in a positive thought or a positive affirmation or meditation, but usually they are the exception to the rule. If we will just envision that maybe we spend an hour a day (and that's probably stretching it) consciously thinking positively and we spend every other waking hour worrying about our problems, it's no wonder we are in such a mess.

Now, I want you to read the following words very carefully. This truth is being revealed at this time not to instill fear in us, but to motivate us into the positive action we are **absolutely capable** of accomplishing.

With the return of the Solar Christ Presence, the Law of Attraction is being greatly accelerated.

This means what we put our attention and energy into is being greatly EMPOWERED. If we are focusing on the Light of Eternal Youth, Vibrant Health, Radiant Beauty, God's Limitless Flow of Abundance, Divine Love, Fulfillment, Happiness, Joy, Eternal Peace, Reverence for All Life, Healing, Limitless Physical Perfection, Planetary Transformation and the Permanent manifestation of Heaven on Earth, then all is well. If, however, we are focusing on the depravity of the lower human ego and all of its potential treachery and destruction, pain and suffering, then we are really in trouble. That negativity will be accelerated into tangible form, thus bringing to fruition the prophecies of old, which profess the virtual obliteration of this Sweet Earth.

> *What we must feel and hear deep within*
> *the recesses of our Heart Flame is that*
> *WE HAVE A CHOICE!*
>
> *AND THAT CHOICE IS...*
> *THE POWER OF OUR ATTENTION!!*

The entire Company of Heaven knows this fact, and so does every Lifestream that is capable of reaching into the Realms of Illumined Truth.

This simple statement is the **KEY to Divine Discerning Intelligence.** It sweeps away all of the obscurities and reveals a pure Pearl of Wisdom that will expose all deception, all misinformation and all ignorance in the Blazing Light of Illumined Truth.

Simply stated, if *any* information, regardless of who the source claims to be (channels, psychics, E.T.s, Masters, etc.), is drawing Humanity's attention to the *negative situations* on Earth in a way that incites fear or worry, then it is *not* from the Realms of Illumined Truth.

Beloved Saint Germain has consistently said, "The greatest means of sorcery on the Planet today is the act of drawing Humanity's attention to negative situations, thus empowering them." If we will be very vigilant and continually monitor our thoughts and feelings, we will be able to clearly determine what we are giving our power to.

Experiment with this knowledge. Whatever you are reading, watching on television, listening to, thinking about, talking about or feeling, ask yourself, *"Is this what I want to be amplifying and creating in my life?"* If it isn't, then say to yourself, *"What do I want instead of this?"* Then, begin thinking about what you want instead. Invoke the Violet Flame of Limitless Transmutation into the negative thoughtform or information being brought to your attention, and Transmute all aspects of it. Refuse to allow your attention to dwell on it, and refuse to empower it with your feelings of fear.

This self-discipline is a critical facet of our self-mastery, and it takes eternal vigilance on our part to succeed. Consistently throughout the day, say to yourself, *"What am I energizing with my thoughts and feelings now? ... and how about now? ...and how about now?"* Initially, it seems like a lot of work, but once you really grasp the importance of the Power of your Attention, you will be very motivated to create only that which adds to the joy of your life and adds to the Light of the World. After all, that's why we are here, to become co-Creators with our Father-Mother God, manifesting the perfection of "As above, so below" ...Heaven on Earth.

Let's not be pawns of the forces of imbalance. Let's not play the game of putting our attention on all of the human miscreation and disinformation they are trying to get us to focus on. Instead of fear, use the Violet Flame of Limitless Transmutation when you hear or read about crime, corruption, war, famines, plagues, cataclysmic Earth changes, destructive weather conditions,

E.T.s, "the grays," the Tri-lateral Commission, "Lizzies," poverty, disease, environmental pollution, inhumanity, animal abuse, forces of imbalance, destructive powers in governments, substance abuse, "big brother," I.R.S., and on and on ad infinitum. We know this negativity exists, but we also know that the only way it is sustained is through the Power of our Attention. It's time for us to stop allowing ourself to be manipulated into co-creating the demise of Planet Earth. Instead, we need to fulfill the Divine Plan we volunteered to bring to fruition when we took our Vows in the Heart of God before this embodiment; this is the Divine Plan for saving this Sweet Earth. We volunteered to assist with every fiber of our Being as She and all Her life Ascend into the Fourth Dimensional Octaves of Limitless Physical Perfection. Through the Power of our Attention, HER VICTORY IS ASSURED!!

REACHING FOR CLARITY

These are very confusing times. At any given moment we can pick up a newsletter, a book, a newspaper, a magazine or turn on the radio or television and find an article or broadcast that tells us the Earth is on the brink of total annihilation. We can read about cataclysmic Earth changes that are destined to destroy the majority of the Earth, Humanity and life as we know it. We can read about Nostradamas' predicted holocaust nuclear war that was to manifest during this time frame. We can read about the corruption and degradation of Human Consciousness that is resulting in the collapse of the Global Economy. We can read about the wrath of God that will purge the Earth of the fallen Human element with brimstone and fire. We can read about the invasion of the destructive Extra-terrestrials that have come to take over the Earth. We can also read about the probability that the destruction of the ozone layer, toxic waste, nuclear fallout, AIDS, disease, pollution of the water and air elements, pesticides, famines, droughts, floods, devitalized food supply, obesity, crime, gangs, drugs, guns, ethnic cleansing, white supremacy, corrupt governments, poverty, war, hate and on and on, will be the inevitable death of all life on Earth.

Now, because of the incredible bombardment of negativity that is being inflicted on us by the media and by souls who are often sincere, but not very illumined, the mass consciousness of Humanity is extremely vulnerable and receptive to octaves of information that are being transmitted to us from the realms of deception. Consequently, we are being used as pawns by the forces of imbalance. These entities that form the psychic-astral realm of deception around the Earth are striving with every fiber of their beings to prevent the Earth from moving into Her next Spiral of Evolution. They don't have the understanding or the intelligence to grasp the fact that they are being given a unique opportunity to move into the Light. They think they are being usurped of their power and destroyed. It is beyond the comprehension of their minds to see that they can actually correct their course and return to their original Divine Intent as Sons and Daughters of God. These wayward entities are souls who have fallen deep into the quagmire of human miscreation and are "lost" in every sense of the word.

But, through the incomparable mercy and compassion of our Father-Mother God, even souls in this consciousness of depravity still have a choice to move into the Light. The problem is, of course, that instead of doing what is necessary to lift themselves into the Light, they are doing everything possible to *prevent* the rest of us from moving into the Light. Because we are under so much stress just trying to cope with the challenges of our everyday life, we are rather fragile and, consequently, we are more gullible and more easily deceived than usual. Everything is being accelerated and, therefore, areas of our life in which we are not reaching our highest potential are coming up in such a way that we can no longer push them down and repress them. We aren't being given the luxury of denial anymore. We are having to address our issues. This is very uncomfortable and scary, but what we must keep reminding ourself of is that these issues are coming up so that we can clear them and be truly FREE. We cannot move into the Octaves of Heaven on Earth with all of our pain and old baggage stuffed down and repressed inside of us.

The fortunate thing is we are receiving more assistance from God and His/Her Messengers in clearing our negativity than ever before in the history of time. There are more Divine Tools being revealed to us and more effective techniques of invoking the Light than ever before. We have the **absolute ability** to move through our personal and Planetary cleansing relatively unscathed. We just need to keep our *attention focused on the Light* and stop allowing ourself to be distracted by the realms of deception.

I would like to share some ideas with you as "food for thought." As I have expressed time and again, I don't want you to ever accept anything as truth just because someone told you it is truth. Instead, I would like you to just allow this information to resonate in the Divinity of your Heart. Ask your God Presence to filter out any trace of human consciousness, and absorb only that which resonates as the truth of your Divine Plan.

The incredible confusion and the misinformation and disinformation we are being bombarded with at this time is not new. At the inception of every New Age, as we move from the forcefield on one constellation and the influence of its Solar Aspect of Deity into the forcefield of a new constellation and a new Solar Aspect of Deity, there is a Cosmic Moment when a unique Window of Opportunity is open between Heaven and Earth. During this brief, but greatly empowered span of time, knowledge and wisdom from the Divine Heart and Mind of God floods the Planet and sets the tone and direction for the next 2000-year cycle. We are now in the midst of an open Window of Opportunity. The Earth is moving from the forcefield of the constellation of Pisces and the Sixth Solar Aspect of Deity, which has influenced us for the past 2000 years, into the forcefield of the constellation of Aquarius and the Seventh Solar Aspect of Deity, which will influence us for the next 2000 years.

During the last open Window of Opportunity, at the inception of the New Age of Pisces 2000 years ago, it was determined by the Godhead that the need of the hour on Earth was to reveal to Humanity the true savior. It was determined that Humanity must heal our self-inflicted separation from our own Divinity, and we must return to our Divine Heritage as Sons and Daughters of God. The Sixth Solar Aspect of Deity flows into the Planet through the constellation of Pisces, and It contains within Its glorious frequencies all that was necessary to bring God's Plan for the Piscean Age to fruition. The Sixth Solar Aspect of Deity pulsates with the God Qualities of Eternal Peace, Devotional Worship, Ministering Grace, Healing and the Consciousness of The Christ made manifest through Humanity.

A magnificent Being of Light volunteered to come to Earth and reveal to Humanity the pathway Home. He embodied as a normal human being to prove, **through example,** that Humanity *can* return to the consciousness of Enlightenment known as The Christ, which is the true SAVIOR of our fallen human ego.

This Divine Being is known to us as Jesus, and he utilized all of the influences of the Window of Opportunity of the New Age of Pisces to assist himself in fulfilling his mission. He was known as the Prince of Peace, which allowed him to continually magnetize the Sixth Solar Aspect of Deity into his Divine Plan, and his symbol was the fish, which drew to him the full momentum of Pisces. He consistently reiterated to Humanity that he had come to show us the way Home to our Father-Mother God. He stated that he was an example, and each human being was capable of accomplishing what he victoriously accomplished. He attained Christ Consciousness and proved the reality of The Christ, which is the Enlightenment that is the true

Son/Daughter of God. He clearly stated that only by Ascending into the consciousness of The Christ will we return to the Heart of our Father-Mother God and, thus, be "saved."

Beloved Jesus continually affirmed throughout his mission of Ministering Grace, "Ye are Gods."

Jesus answered them, "Is it not written in your law, I said, 'YE ARE GODS'?"   John 10:34

"YE ARE GODS, and all of you ARE children of the most High."   Psalms 82:6

"Verily, verily, I say unto you, he that believeth in me, the works that I do shall he do also, AND EVEN GREATER WORKS THAN THESE SHALL HE DO..."   John 14:12

"For as many as are led by the Spirit of God, they are the Sons of God - the Spirit itself beareth witness with our spirit that we are the Children of God; and if Children, then Heirs, Heirs of God, JOINT HEIRS WITH CHRIST.."   Romans 8:14 -17

"When I consider Thy Heavens, the work of Thy fingers, the moon and the stars which Thou hast ordained; what is man, that Thou art mindful of him and the son of man, that Thou visitest him? For Thou hast made him a little lower than the angels and has crowned him with glory and honor. Thou madest him TO HAVE DOMINION OVER THE WORKS OF THY HANDS; THOU HAST PUT ALL THINGS UNDER HIS FEET."
Psalms 8:3-6

Even though Jesus continually reiterated our worth and stated, *"It is not I, but the Father within Who does the work,"* we still misunderstood his message and once again separated ourself from him, deified him, and worshiped him, which was never the original Divine Intent.

Through the open Window of Opportunity of Pisces, Jesus brought to Earth the Law of Forgiveness. Prior to the inception of the Piscean Age, the Earth operated under the Law of Jehovah, which was *"An eye for an eye, a tooth for a tooth."* This is the Law of Karma, the law of cause and effect. With the renewal of the consciousness of Enlightenment, The Christ, the Law of Forgiveness was set into motion on Earth. Now, instead of having to wade through the painful effects of our misqualified thoughts, words, actions and feelings, we can ask to be forgiven and Transmute the effects PRIOR to the time we have to experience them as a painful situation in our life. Because of this compassionate gift from God, Jesus was said to have forgiven the sins of the World.

Now, after having read the previous information, let's observe how the forces of imbalance and the realms of deception interfered and confused us by turning our attention to fear and the negativity on Earth. During the open Window of Opportunity of Pisces 2000 years ago, the religious leaders, clinging to their distorted literal interpretation of Holy Scripture, came up with their idea of who the "Messiah" was and what he would do. They determined what they thought needed to be done from their prejudiced, limited, judgmental perspective and declared it law. They stated just what was going to occur when the "Messiah" came and what he would do, according to their expectations. Well, as is *always* the case, God's Plan is infinitely more splendid than anything our finite human minds can conceive. Consequently, when the Messiah came in a way that was far more normal, yet tremendously more powerful than what the religious leaders were expecting, they actually missed the whole event. We have been struggling ever since to try and figure out what the life of Jesus and his teachings really meant.

Now, we are on the dawn of the New Age of Aquarius, and we are receiving the Blessings of the Seventh Solar Aspect of Deity, which reverberates with the Violet Flame of Limitless

Transmutation, Forgiveness, Mercy, Compassion, Freedom, Liberty, Invocation, Justice and Victory. A new Window of Opportunity is opening. As the knowledge and wisdom from the Divine Heart and Mind of God begin to flood the Planet, crumbling our distorted belief systems and challenging our realities, we see the realms of deception clamoring for center stage.

Once again the religious leaders of the day are trying to project their distorted beliefs and their misinterpretation of the Holy Scriptures onto the screen of life as law. Through the fear of loss of control of their congregations, they are intensifying their efforts to block the truth, which they feel conflicts with their teachings. They are professing that the wisdom and knowledge now pouring forth from the Divine Heart and Mind of God is the "work of the devil," and they are trying to crucify the truth just as the religious leaders crucified Jesus in the last **New Age**.

Fortunately, this time it is different. This time we are truly healing our self-inflicted separation from our own Divinity. We are experiencing an awakening, and we are lifting up in consciousness in a way that allows us to have ***Divine Discerning Intelligence*** and a new order of ***Reason.*** We are now able to observe what we are seeing and hearing through the eyes and ears of ***Common Sense,*** clearly and truthfully. As we invoke the clarity of ***Divine Discerning Intelligence, Reason*** and ***Common Sense*** into our perceptions and experiences, we will see and know the TRUTH of this Cosmic Moment.

Please invoke those Divine Qualities as you evaluate the following concepts.

One of the most distorted and most destructive deceptions being inflicted on Humanity is **the belief that Jesus did it all for us**. If anything keeps us trapped and bound in limitation, it is the lies of the psychic-astral plane that say, *"Don't even bother to try. You are a worthless sinner. You can never reach a Christlike state of perfection. Because you are such a failure, God sent His* *only Son to save you. No matter how depraved or destructive you are, if you will just mumble the worlds 'I accept Jesus as my personal savior,' all is forgiven, and you will be in Heaven forever. If you don't say those words, you will burn in hell for all Eternity. You are so hopeless that Jesus had to die for **your** sins. Just be grateful to Him, and continue your miserable existence."*

This dimension of deception actually has the audacity to tell us that it is blasphemous for us to believe that we can return to Christ Consciousness and become The Christ as Jesus taught us we could, when, in fact, returning to Christ Consciousness is the **only** way we heal our separation from our God Self, and it is what the Second Coming of The Christ is all about.

The Second Coming of The Christ is not Jesus riding into the atmosphere of Earth on a white cloud rapturing the few who have said the words, "I accept Jesus as my personal saviour," into an ethereal state of bliss, regardless of how degenerate or depraved they may be, while he casts everyone else who has not said those words into a tortuous, burning hell for all Eternity, REGARDLESS OF HOW LOVING AND CHRISTLIKE THEIR LIVES MAY HAVE BEEN . (Now would be a good time to interject some common sense.)

The Second Coming of The Christ is *every* man, woman and child *emulating* and *becoming* the expression of Love and Enlightenment that Jesus taught us we *must* BE in order to return to our Father-Mother God.

That has nothing to do with ego. It is merely fulfilling our purpose and reason for being.

Let's look at this from another perspective. We are *all* saying that one day Heaven will manifest on Earth and the Universal Law of "As above, so below" will be a reality. This means Eternal Peace, Vibrant Health, Limitless Physical Perfection, Abundance, Loving Relationships, Joy, Happiness, etc. Now, in order for that level of perfection to be sustained on Earth, *everyone* abiding here has to have the Consciousness of Reverence for ALL Life, Tolerance, Divine Love, Acceptance, Compassion and every other attribute of God. In your experience, have the people you know who have said the words, "I accept Jesus as my personal savior" attained that level of Consciousness? In my experience, it has been quite the opposite, and the reason is because they truly believe that they are incapable of it. They, therefore, keep themselves trapped and bound in the "worthless sinner" state of consciousness. **Remember, we become who we believe we are.**

For us to be sitting around waiting to be raptured instead of striving with every fiber of our Being to become The Christ through the path of Divine Love as Jesus taught us, is a grave error in judgment. If ANYTHING is the so-called *"work of the devil,"* it is perpetuating the belief that Jesus did it for us, and all we have to do is accept him as our "savior."

He *saved* us in that he showed us the way into Christ Consciousness and brought the Law of Forgiveness to Earth. But, we are only "saved" if we **apply** the knowledge and wisdom he brought to us and BECOME THE CHRIST. We are not saved just because he was here on Earth or because *he* became The Christ. To believe that is the equivalent of going to the university and listening to our professor who has earned his Ph.D., then telling everyone we have a Ph.D. also, just because our teacher earned his degree, even though we haven't done any of the necessary work to earn our *own* Ph.D.

The lie that states Jesus did it all for us is working very effectively to entrap millions of "Born Again" Christians and Christians of other orthodox religions as well. The lie that states the Messiah is coming soon and will do it all for us when he gets here is another aspect of the same erroneous belief system, which is also entrapping millions of additional souls in stagnation.

Now, there is another scenario from the psychic-astral realm of deception that is being projected into the minds of awakening souls all over the Planet, and it is having the same effect o entrapment and stagnation. This ploy of deception is being aimed at the souls who are perceived to be more open-minded, and it is using, of all things, the most sacred aspect of this Cosmic Moment, the Ascension. The disinformation is indicating that there will be various "waves" of Ascension, and as souls awaken and volunteer for this Ascension, they will be physically lifted off the Planet onto spaceships. There, they will be taught to be Ascended Masters as the Earth is purged with cataclysmic Earth changes, Earthquakes and various other holocausts. Then, they will be put back on Earth as Superhuman Beings, and they will *"save,"* through their teachings, anyone who is still surviving on Earth after the "cleansing."

Even though this scenario is using more modern terminology to deceive the more open-minded souls, the concept behind it is identical to the rapture. It is still saying someone else is doing it for us, and somehow we will be miraculously "saved" by an outside force. Well, guess what? No such luck! I know initially it feels really scary to think our salvation and the salvation of the Planet is up to us, but IT IS!!! ***The good news is that we have the absolute ability to pull this thing off.*** If we will just stop waiting to be raptured or lifted off or destroyed by cataclysms or victimized by Humanity's frailty, we can do it. We have been prepared for thousands of years to be on Earth during this moment to assist in Her rebirth, and we have all of the skill, talent, wisdom and courage we need to do it. We just need to **act** NOW.

I think it will help if we go back to some of the basics of why we are here on Earth in the first place during this unprecedented time. First of all, we must remember that in order for something to manifest in the physical plane, the unformed primal Light substance must be drawn through the creative faculties of thought and feeling of someone abiding in the physical plane. In other words, God and the entire Company of Heaven cannot change what is occurring on Earth from the higher dimensions of Perfection.   If that could happen, They would have transformed the human miscreation aeons ago. The only way transformation can occur is by souls who live on Earth invoking the Light of God that is Eternally Victorious through their Heart Flames and projecting It into the physical plane through their thoughts, words, actions and feelings. This, then, makes the Light of Transformation available for all life evolving on Earth. We must actually be transformers, instruments, to transmit the Light from the Heart of God into the physical plane of Earth. This Light contains within It the Divine Momentum of Healing, and every other Quality of God. It has the ability to Transmute negativity and restore physical matter. It can shift consciousness and awaken Humanity. It can transform and rejuvenate; It can assist us in remembering who we are and why we are here. **But**, unless someone living on Earth invokes the Light of God into this dimension and allows It to flow through their Heart Flame into the world of form, there is **no way we can benefit from all of Its Blessings.**

So, all of these scenarios that profess the Lightworkers or "good people" will be taken off the Planet during the cleansing **can't possibly be true.** After all, we volunteered to be here in physical embodiment, so we could be instruments and transmitters of Light during this critical time. We volunteered to be here to invoke the Light of God into Humanity's consciousness, so the masses will awaken and remember that they are Sons and Daughters of God and begin acting out of that Divinity. We volunteered to be here to invoke the Light of Divine Love, Healing, Prosperity, Peace, Joy, Happiness, Limitless Physical Perfection, Forgiveness, Transmutation, Transformation, Truth, Illumination and every other God Quality that will enable Beloved Mother Earth to move through the birthing process **gently and harmoniously.**

Why in the world, after thousands of years of training and preparation at both inner and outer levels, would we agree to *cop-out* and *split* at the moment we have been preparing for aeons of time—the very moment when we will be needed the most? Well, it makes no sense at all, and it is merely the interference of the psychic-astral realm that is trying to distract us from our mission.

I know many Lightworkers who are being tricked into believing this drivel, and they have actually stopped their Lightwork and are sitting around waiting for lift-off. What a tragic disservice!

Come on, Precious Ones, hear the **wake-up call** reverberating from the Heart of our Father-Mother God. Let's remember who we are and why we are here. IT IS NOT TOO LATE!!! This is the moment we have been waiting for. **Your Light and Love are needed now!**

Listen to your Heart. Respond to the Divine Opportunities being presented to you every day of your life. Ask yourself with every breath you take, *"How, this moment, can I add to the Light and Healing of the World, the Earth, the Elemental Kingdom, Humanity, my Family, my Loved Ones and Myself?"* Then **ACT** on the inner, intuitive feelings and ideas you have. Your God Presence is anxiously waiting to guide you into the greatest God Victorious Mission you have ever undertaken. This is going to be the most exciting, rewarding, fulfilling, wonderful, awesome experience we have ever encountered since we were first breathed forth from the Core of Creation. I promise you, leaving the Earth at the moment of Her most glorious Victory would be a tragic anti-climax.

I just want to add one more word of encouragement. The reason we have been so easily deceived is because this realm of deception knows we are not stupid. Consequently, these masters of deceit say what we want to hear. They always use the names of our Beloved Spiritual Hierarchy because they know we trust these Divine Beings of Light. What often happens is that we see a message that claims to be from Saint Germain or Mother Mary or Jesus, etc., and we assume it must be true. The channels are often very sincere, so we just accept what we are being told. THIS IS A TIME WHEN WE MUST **NOT**

CONFUSE SINCERITY WITH TRUTH.

We must ignore who the message is supposed to be from, and focus solely on the content of the message. Blaze the Flame of Truth through every word, and invoke **Divine Discerning Intelligence, Common Sense** and **Reason**. Then, put the message to the ultimate test. Knowing that the Law of Attraction means **what we put our attention and energy into, we bring into form,** ask yourself, *"Is this what I want to be creating on Earth?"* If the message is focusing on cataclysmic Earth changes, destruction, fear, negative things that are happening on Earth or the woes of Humanity, then it is NOT coming from the true Spiritual Hierarchy. These Divine Beings KNOW that our most important mission is manifesting the perfection of Heaven on Earth. Thus, They perpetually turn our attention to the reality of our own Divinity, our Limitless multi-dimensional Self, Who is a co-Creator with our Father-Mother God. They project into our Heart and Mind the Divine Blueprint of the New Heaven and the New Earth, and They continually hold, before our mind's eye, the Immaculate Concept of this Sweet Earth and all Her life transformed into...FREEDOM'S HOLY STAR. Their messages are obvious. They are filled with Hope, Encouragement, Trust, Joy, Elation, Gratitude and, above all, the assurance of God's Victorious Accomplishment in the unparalleled mission we have all now embarked upon.

Oh, how very, very Blessed we are to be part of this Divine Adventure!!!

Thank You! Thank You! Thank You!
Beloved Father-Mother God!

CHAPTER
TWELVE

KEYNOTE VISUALIZATION

BECOMING ALL "I AM"

Breathing rhythmically and deeply, I greet this sacred day from within the peace of my liberated God Presence on Earth. Centered here I feel one with all life, and I now realize that "I Am" all Humanity standing forth as the Arisen Solar Christ. I feel an upward rushing force of the Ascension of Humanity's *free will* back to the Christ. All *free will* is Ascending into the Realm of Limitless Physical Perfection for this Sweet Star of Freedom. In this meditation, I now stretch into and accept the Infinity of my own God Consciousness, all of which I claim here in the physical vehicle. But "I Am" also all of Humanity, and I feel Her Infinity Consciousness as the Stargate of Her Heart opens Globally. I dwell in the peace of my personal and Global God expression, and I know "All things are in Divine Order."

Standing forth within my Solar Twelve-fold Flame, I begin to profoundly experience God Power on all planes. I experience my Divine Integrity, knowing my Presence on Earth as but one Aspect of my Infinity Consciousness. In this awakening, "I Am" now a **Universal Instrument on Earth**. As I inbreathe and absorb the Flaming Presence of Light streaming into my Heart, I know myself on many levels. "I Am" the Celestial Christ Self in the Perfected Realms of Planet Earth, performing my Cosmic Service of Loving free all lesser energies. I find my gentle rhythm in this Aspect of my Divinity, and "I Am" that "I Am". Then, my awareness increases into the Mighty "I Am" Presence into the Electronic Realms around the Sun. Here I experience myself as a Cosmic Flame with Light Rays radiating out in all directions of the Universe. I know myself as God in Action...here, there and everywhere present. As the rhythm of this Aspect of my Divinity anchors into the core of my physical Being, I again know "I Am" that "I Am". I, then, further Ascend along my Solar Silver Cord into the Galactic Presence of my White Fire Being within the Great Central Sun. Here "I Am" whole, my full Masculine and Feminine God Self as one glorious Being of Light. Here I see, feel and become part of the service of our glorious Great Central Sun, Alpha and Omega. Here I also begin to experience the Great, Great Central Sun of Elohae and Eloha. I experience the endless Ocean of Light and the great Infinity of Suns beyond Suns beyond Suns...and I know "I Am" that "I Am". Here I rest in Eternity.

Yet, on the very same breath, in this moment of timelessness, I also experience this Ocean of Infinity *within the Solar Atoms composing my physical vehicle.* I live within the very Eternity that I seek. I now experience my entire physical presence as a Solar Atom. I see and feel my Twelve-fold Flame as the nucleus. The periphery of my atom is my Electronic Aura. All the energies of my four lower vehicles now exist in the Divine Fourth Dimensional space within the atom which "I Am". I have now become collectively what each of my atoms expresses individually. I see and feel each of these atoms and my entire physical presence as **Divine Instruments of Endless Light** in service here on Earth. In this one breath, I have realized that "I Am" simultaneously every aspect of Divine life along the Silver Cord, from the Highest Electronic Realms within the Great, Great Central Sun through to the atoms expressing here in the physical plane. And I accept now all that "I Am" *here in my physical body.*

I now experience the Celestial Aura of my entire Infinity Consciousness...my **Causal Body**. It envelops all that "I Am" in a great multi-colored, multi-dimensional Sea of dazzling Light. These Spheres of Glory around me are all the Divine Blessings which I have ever generated—every good and perfect thought, feeling and action I have ever created in my service to God **on any plane of existence**. All that "I Am" as a White Fire Being, as an "I Am" Presence, as a Solar Christ Self now envelops me as a great Celestial Aura of the many Dimensions and Solar Aspects of God. This Causal Body enfolds every

Aspect of my Being, including every physical atom. I pause now and feel this deeply within my body.

My Causal Body is really the Limitless Realms of *my own Universe unfolding.* For "I Am" a potential Sun God or Goddess, someday possibly to parent my own Universe of Divine Life. This Solar Causal Body is "my treasures stored in Heaven," and I now assimilate all of this into my physical life on Earth. For "I Am" that "I Am", here and now! And with every breath, I flood the world with the countless Spheres of Perfection that "I Am".

Connecting all of these Aspects of my Divine Being is a great River of Cosmic Light, my Solar Silver Cord. As I breathe slowly and deeply, I gently become just this River of Divine Light, flowing from Infinity to Infinity. It may express Itself as the various Aspects of my Divine Self. But I may also choose to know myself *only as this Celestial River of endless Light,* and "I Am" that "I Am". "I Am" the River of Light. "I Am" the Ocean of Infinity *from* which It flows, and "I Am" the Ocean of Infinity *into* which It flows. This River of Light is made up of perfection Particles and perfection Light Waves, all of which constitute my Divine Creation flowing through the Universe...my Cosmic Thread in the Celestial Tapestry of the Great Solar Day. "I Am" Creation's endless expansion.

In becoming this Celestial River of Light, I now understand my Infinity Consciousness and claim every Aspect of my Divine Being along Its "banks" into my *physical* Spiritual Freedom. For this Cosmic River of Light may now flow unimpeded through my Christed physical Body of Light. "I Am" now releasing into the Light all thoughts, feelings and memories less than this Immaculate Concept of myself. "I Am" embodied on Earth to express my *free will choice* to function as a Divine Instrument of Service and to experience the joy of physical perfection. But, all that "I Am", all the God Perfection that flows along my Solar Silver Cord is here with me now, and I let it **blaze forth into the physical realm.** "I Am" at peace in the physical realm.

Resting now in the Supreme God Confidence of Infinity Consciousness manifesting on Earth, I feel the opening of the Stargate of the Heart. I immediately see the Truth of Life all around me. Once again I see all imbalanced energies as they were to be seen in the expanded Divine Plan...innocent primordial Light entering my awareness to be redeemed. I now greet all imbalanced energies as would the God Parents from within the Flame of Peace, Detachment, God Confidence and Supreme Authority. I take this energy into my Being, holding it in my arms of Light as I would an injured child. I do not let it overwhelm me or control me, nor do I need to fear it or shun it. I simply hold it and Love it...until it has calmed, desiring on its own part to rejoin the Kingdom of Heaven, *which is within me!* As this energy releases itself into the Light, it experiences the Infinity Consciousness, which "I Am". And it may again find its proper place in the Universe. It shall now be Eternally Free, with all things in Divine Order. I affirm to all life everywhere:

"Come unto me
and be raised up into the Father-Mother God."

"Come unto me
and be raised up into the Father-Mother God."

"Come unto me
and be raised up into the Father-Mother God."

As this practice grows more rhythmic and established in my day-to-day life, I realize "I Am" in Holy Communion...the constant Communion of my Father God and my Mother God within me, expressing now as the Christ "I Am". I experience the Holy Communion of all of my energies around my Flame...all of my will becoming God's Will...all of my Love becoming God's Love...all of my Being becoming God's Being. I experience my full Solar Integrity, my full Solar Ancestry, as **the Harmony of my True Being!**....the Communion of all my energies within my Flame, on every level of my Infinite Being. This Communion includes all of what "I Am" in the Electronic Realms of the White Fire Being, in the Ascended Master Realms as the "I Am" Presence, in the Fourth Dimensional Realms as the Solar Christ Awakening on Earth *and all the unascended energies of my physical embodiment.* All of what "I Am", Ascended and unascended, is now dancing around my Heart Flame, assimilated into my physical being with every breath, every Heartbeat, every action that I take. I now take every aspect, every atom of my life's energies with me along the Great Cosmic Inbreath into Eternity.

As the Harmony of my True Being sustains my Ultimate Protection, I know that I can safely accept unascended energies into myself as an Instrument of Transformation. Rather than feeling rejected and thus lingering as patterns of disease and distress, these energies will, instead, feel accepted, held in Love and Revered as the innate God Energy they are. They will then voluntarily release themselves into the Light, into all the Great Forcefields and Momentums of Light "I Am". For "I Am" the full Power of the Mother God in Action doing this. The Father God is my ability to stretch into Infinity, and the Mother God is my ability to be with this energy until it chooses Freedom. My Holy Communion is the unity of all my Ascended Forcefields and Momentums with all my own unascended energies and all impersonal laggard energies I have volunteered to redeem on this Planet. All of this is now taking place within my physical presence on Earth as a great *Dance of Transformation* within me. I both participate in this dance and observe it in the detached peace of the Great "I Am". The present Cosmic Moment on Earth is taking place right inside my embodied vehicles...and I know the Light of God is always Victorious.

I remain in harmony within the Father God's Confidence, Protection and God Authority and the Mother God's Love,

Patience and Divine Compassion as They Commune together in Their Sacred Dance within me...out of which comes the Resurrection and Ascension of my full Christ Being, physically expressing on Earth. I rejoice in my service of allowing my White Fire Being, my Mighty "I Am" Presence and my Solar Christ Self Their Sacred Service on Earth through these vehicles. And I rejoice that unascended energy will now find its way Home through me. I release myself into the peace of knowing:

"My Perfection is handling ALL imperfection Perfectly."

"My Perfection is handling ALL imperfection Perfectly."

"My Perfection is handling ALL imperfection Perfectly."

From Group Avatar.

Note: For more information regarding Group Avatar, you may write to:

Group Avatar
P.O.Box 41505
Tucson, Arizona 85717-1505

AVAILABLE BOOKS AND TAPES
by Patricia Diane Cota-Robles

TAKE CHARGE OF YOUR LIFE

THE NEXT STEP...Re-Unification With The Presence of God Within Our Hearts

*YOUR TIME IS AT HAN*D

THE AWAKENING...Eternal Youth, Vibrant Health, Radiant Beauty

STARGATE OF THE HEART

Each of the above books has a corresponding set of audio cassette tapes to help you absorb and effectively experience the Sacred Knowledge pouring forth from the Realms of Illumined Truth.

For a catalogue of available books and tapes and a FREE sample of the newsletter *Take Charge of Your Life,* just fill in the coupon below and mail it to:

The New Age Study of Humanity's Purpose
PO Box 41883
Tucson AZ 85717
FAX 602-751-3835

Please send me the catalogue of available books and tapes by Patricia Diane Cota-Robles and a sample of the newsletter *Take Charge of Your Life.*

*NAME*_____

*ADDRESS*_____

*CITY*_____*STATE*_____*ZIP*_____

*COUNTRY*_____

AVAILABLE BOOKS AND TAPES
by Patricia Diane Cota-Robles

TAKE CHARGE OF YOUR LIFE

THE NEXT STEP...Re-Unification With The Presence of God Within Our Hearts

YOUR TIME IS AT HAND

THE AWAKENING...Eternal Youth, Vibrant Health, Radiant Beauty

STARGATE OF THE HEART

Each of the above books has a corresponding set of audio cassette tapes to help you absorb and effectively experience the Sacred Knowledge pouring forth from the Realms of Illumined Truth.

For a catalogue of available books and tapes and a FREE sample of the newsletter *Take Charge of Your Life,* just fill in the coupon below and mail it to:

The New Age Study of Humanity's Purpose
PO Box 41883
Tucson AZ 85717
FAX 602-751-3835

Please send me the catalogue of available books and tapes by Patricia Diane Cota-Robles and a sample of the newsletter *Take Charge of Your Life.*

*NAME*_____

*ADDRESS*_____

*CITY*_____*STATE*_____*ZIP*_____

*COUNTRY*_____

AVAILABLE BOOKS AND TAPES
by Patricia Diane Cota-Robles

TAKE CHARGE OF YOUR LIFE

THE NEXT STEP...Re-Unification With The Presence of God Within Our Hearts

YOUR TIME IS AT HAND

THE AWAKENING...Eternal Youth, Vibrant Health, Radiant Beauty

STARGATE OF THE HEART

Each of the above books has a corresponding set of audio cassette tapes to help you absorb and effectively experience the Sacred Knowledge pouring forth from the Realms of Illumined Truth.

For a catalogue of available books and tapes and a FREE sample of the newsletter *Take Charge of Your Life,* just fill in the coupon below and mail it to:

The New Age Study of Humanity's Purpose
PO Box 41883
Tucson AZ 85717
FAX 602-751-3835

Please send me the catalogue of available books and tapes by Patricia Diane Cota-Robles and a sample of the newsletter *Take Charge of Your Life.*

*NAME*_____

*ADDRESS*_____

*CITY*_____*STATE*_____*ZIP*_____

*COUNTRY*_____